STEELHEAD FLOAT FISHING

Jim Butler

STEELHEAD
FLOAT FISHING

Jim Butler

Book Dedication

This book is dedicated to the memory of Kevin Jenkins. Kevin, an avid angler, was sadly taken from us after a snowy day of early spring steelhead fishing. His untimely passing continues to echo within and throughout.

This manuscript is also dedicated to those devoted steelheaders who find the time each year to roll up their sleeves and actively partake in their local stream rehabilitation efforts.

Steelheaders who embark on such endeavors have my sincerest respect for it is they who realize the true essence of angling.

Acknowledgments

A book of this nature could simply not exist as a result of one's own individual effort, therefore I would like to express my sincerest thanks and gratitude to the following for all their contributions.

A very special thanks to Jon George, Senior Fisheries Specialist with the Ontario Ministry of Natural Resources, for shedding light on the life history characteristics of Lake Superior and Great Lakes steelhead.

I would also like to extend my thanks to the many Great Lakes steelhead biologists who also provided valuable information for this text. Thanks to Douglas Dodge, Jim Bowlby, Dennis Pratt, Bill Blust, Paul Seelbach, David Swank and Mark Bere (Department of Fisheries and Oceans).

Special thanks also to Chris Atkinson, founder of the Nottawasaga Steelheaders for schooling me on the merits of wild verses hatchery steelhead and also for introducing me to Jon George. Thanks for also introducing me to some prime Nottawasaga steelhead water.

Thanks to Paul Shimano for encouraging me to build my own tackle, Tina Tincher from the institute for Fisheries Research, Barry Stokes from Islander Reels and Tom McMurray from Normark Rapala for all their help and contributions. I would also like to express my thanks to the Amato Family for providing me with a voice in which to express my ideologies to the Great Lakes steelhead fraternity.

Of course where would any of us be without the love and support of family. My sincerest thanks to my mother for raising me as a single parent and for tolerating my passion for angling throughout my youth.

Thanks to Kim Butler for painstakingly typing this manuscript and for waking up at ungodly hours to help photograph some of its contents.

Thanks to Ted McNally for all of his artistic contributions. Also to my Uncle Sid and "Popeye" Butler (grandfather) for instilling in me a love for the great outdoors.

About the Author

Jim Butler has been pursuing steelhead from around the Great Lakes since the early 1980s. As a result of his profound interest and observations, many of his articles have been published throughout the angling community. His work has appeared in such magazines as Ontario Fisherman, Ontario Out of Doors and Salmon, Trout, Steelheader—just to name a few.

During the brief off season Jim can still be found streamside as he divides his time participating in local stream rehabilitation projects as well as studying steelhead fry interactions and aquatic entomology.

Jim also manages time each season to supply his local tackle shops with his quality steelhead floats and jigs.

His other interests include researching food chain communities of the Great Lakes, and writing and playing crazy eights with his goddaughter and niece.

©2004 by Jim Butler
All rights reserved. No part of this book may be reproduced without the written consent of the publisher,
except in the case of brief excerpts in critical reviews and articles.

All inquiries should be addressed to:
Frank Amato Publications, Inc. • P.O. Box 82112 • Portland, Oregon 97282
503-653-8108 • www.amatobooks.com

Photography: Jim Butler unless noted
Book Design: Jerry Hutchinson
ISBN: 1-57188-322-3
UPC: 0-81127-00156-9
Printed in Singapore
1 3 5 7 9 10 8 6 4 2

Introduction 6

Life Histories, Strategies, and Behaviors 8

Steelhead Water 19

Fishing with Floats 24

Natural and Artificial Baits 31

Autumn Steelhead 40

Winter Steelhead 52

Spring Steelhead 60

Involvement and the Future 66

Float Reels and How to Cast Them 68

Building Balsa Floats 72

Chinook Salmon 74

Bibliography 78

Introduction

Take a look down any stream in the Great Lakes region during the autumn or spring steelhead season and one thing becomes inherently clear—the majority of anglers have adopted to float fishing to help them produce consistent catches of migrating steelhead.

Float fishing, over all other methods and presentations, is perhaps responsible for more hooked steelhead throughout the Great Lakes tributaries than any other fishing technique. This, however, is not to say that using alternative techniques to capture steelhead is not productive because nothing could be further from the truth. It does suggest though, that implementing the use of floats to deliver our suspended presentation is by far the most lucrative and prolific method to consistently connect with returning runs of Great Lakes steelhead.

So just why is float fishing so much more productive over most, if not all other angling methods, when it comes to catching steelhead? The simple answer is because floats offer us controlled depth fishing. Floats allow us to suspend our presentations at the same stream level where seasonal steelhead choose to locate. Drifting float presentations through productive steelhead lies however, is only a small part of what is required to become a more prolific steelheader.

Understanding steelhead behavior—their woes and whims through migratory seasons and water conditions—is perhaps the single most important factor which can lead to a steelheader's success.

When I first began pursuing steelhead back in the early 1980s I was like most others who were first starting out. My early attempts to catch them under the float were futile. Intrigued, rather than discouraged by my lack of success, I soon began to set goals. First I vowed never to leave the river without having learned at least one new detail about the habitual nature of returning steelhead. Secondly, I had to acquire my driver's license so I would no longer have to walk to and from my local river with waders, tackle and frozen extremities.

Inspired by their behavior and my quest to produce daily results, I soon began to delve deeper into the biological influences that surround our migratory steelhead. Once I began to understand how steelhead were regulated by their ever-changing environments and how they interconnected with other organisms within their environment, I soon began to fulfill my objective of consistent catches.

Today, armed with the knowledge that I have accumulated over the last two decades, I can literally guarantee myself daily hookups at whichever Great Lakes watershed I decide to frequent. Do I ever get bored having reached this plateau? Absolutely not! Today, I am even more intrigued than ever because I fish not to see how many steelhead I can catch but rather to see which presentations I can fool fish on next and under which circumstance do baits become most productive.

In *Float Fishing for Great Lakes Steelhead*, not only do I disclose all of the steelhead observations that I have made over the last twenty plus years, but I also explore the multitude of natural and artificial presentations that have led to my successes.

Drifting natural baits such as skeined roe sacs beneath a sensitive float is the most popular bait choice of the Great Lakes steelhead fraternity. Although a chapter has been dedicated on how to best scrape and freeze mature skeined eggs, I must say here and now that eggs, in my humble opinion, are often an over utilized, overestimated bait choice. This isn't to say that I do not use roe, only that I have discovered on my own and through friends that there are many more productive artificial alternatives that produce fish on a consistent basis. If the truth be known, I take more fish on artificials each season than I do on roe.

Once you flip through the following pages and discover the merits of artificials I am sure you will find yourself leaving your roe in the fridge a lot more, eventually cutting back on roe use all together.

Whether you are just starting to pursue steelhead or are dyed-in-the-wool, whether you're stuck fishing high and turbid water or low and clear conditions, whether you fish in the dead of winter or the dead of night, this book will guide you through each seasonal steelhead scenario and put you onto productive steelhead water using no-fail time proven techniques.

Aside from learning the when, where, why and hows of becoming a more prolific angler, I have also included a few chapters related to steelhead fishing that are sure to spark interest among the steelhead fraternity.

For those intrigued by the biological aspects of our Great Lakes steelhead, you should find the first chapter a plethora of information. Here, with the help of various Great Lakes biologists, the Department of Fisheries and Oceans and the International North Pacific Fishery Commission, and others, I have included the steelhead's life history from egg to adult, from species to repeat spawning, from feeding to homing, from migration to large growth strategies and beyond.

For those who have recently purchased their first float reel, you may have discovered that the hefty price tag did not include a "how to" booklet on casting. Not to worry as I have also included a chapter on how to properly cast your investment without bothersome backlashes or line twists.

Although casting with a float reel and trying to achieve distance may seem a little difficult at first, I am sure my easy to follow instructions should help straighten the learning curve.

Crafty steelheaders who find they have some spare time during the brief off season will be glad to find that I have also included a chapter on how to build your own balsa floats. A few common household tools are all that's required to make your own custom crafted floats. My easy to follow step by step instructions will take you through the entire float building process.

Since steelhead do not begin their autumn runs until mid to late September across many of the Great Lakes regions, why not get your fishing fix in late summer while targeting the inshore movements of pre-spawn Chinook salmon. If conditions are right, Chinooks can be easily taken off piers and breakwalls often much earlier than most anglers realize. Targeting Chinooks from shore is sure to fill the void while you wait for those first arriving autumn steelhead.

Another way to help pass the time in-between steelhead seasons is to learn all you can about this magnificent sport fishery. If the truth be known, most successful steelheaders I know are successful because they have done their homework. Not only that but they have done it better than most. Consider this manuscript a pleasurable homework assignment and I promise that once you complete it, you will be armed with enough knowledge to join the ranks of those local steelheaders who manage consistent results throughout all seasons and most water conditions.

My hopes are that this manuscript will help you become a more prolific, informed, educated and conservation minded steelheader. I also hope you have as much fun learning from this manuscript as I have had living it.

And please support local stream rehabilitation efforts.

Chapter 1
Steelhead Life Histories Strategies, and Behaviors

The stream was rather small as far as steelhead water goes, however the midsummer droughts that had been plaguing the Great Lakes Region for the past number of summers was partially to blame.

Wadding along the margins of the stream was a lot easier than trying to walk through the vegetated masses that awaited us onshore as we searched for yet another stretch of stream in need of a little improved-access work. (This, in turn, helps ensure future runs of trout and salmon unimpeded access to the holy high grounds.)

As we wadded upstream a splash in the pool above us caught our attention. Intrigued, we waited to see if the young yearling trout would repeat its aerial attempt to secure his midday meal and without fail the young parr marked trout zeroed in on another helpless emerger, gulped it in, then returned to defend its territorial feeding lie.

Observing the young steelhead made me wonder at the many life changes that would transform it from a young parr marked yearling, to a silvery smolt, then eventually into adulthood, and on to its first spawning run as to the same stream in which it had been born.

Since the early-1870s Great Lakes introduction, steelhead have captured the attention of anglers on many levels.

For some, pursuing steelhead from around the Great Lakes has become a passion, however, it has become an obsession for many more. Despite driving rains, cold winds, pelting sleet, blowing snow and frozen extremities, our obsession is unrivaled by the elements as only the diminishing light of day can send us homeward. But such obsession does not just happen and rarely does it come by chance. In most cases it is born. I bet if a survey was to be conducted on how most anglers first became introduced to fishing, they would say that a family member introduced them to the sport, and through those early streamside introductions, a love was born that over the years grew into passion, and was eventually elevated to an obsession.

Those who were introduced to the sport a little later in life will undoubtedly share in the same enthusiasm which stems from pursuing the majestic steelhead. Nevertheless, no matter how you were introduced to the art of steelhead fishing, there is undoubtedly much to learn about these fascinating animals not only from an angling perspective, but from a biological perspective as well.

→ The Races ←

Great Lakes steelhead are direct descendants of the West Coast populations that were imported over 125 years ago. Although many peaks and valleys accompanied their populations throughout the years, it is evident today that they have firmly established localized populations.

Like their West Coast counterparts there are two races of steelhead throughout the Great Lakes. Fish from both regions, however, have expressed varying migration schedules each of which appears to be conducive to environmental conditioning and local adaptations. Steelhead of the Pacific Northwest seemed to have adapted to summer and winter run regimes while steelhead populations of the Great Lakes seemed to have adapted to autumn through spring migrations.

Winter runs exist throughout the Great Lakes during relatively mild winters or during periods of mid-winter thaws, however, these fish may simply be late running autumn or early running spring fish. Questions often arise as to why the Great Lakes population seems to have both autumn and spring migrations if fish do not spawn until spring. The simple answer to that may be because our steelhead have maintained their West Coast genetic lineage despite being stocked throughout the Great Lakes. Steelhead of the Pacific Coast have adapted to varying run times because they need to traverse greater distances, overcoming natural barriers prior to reaching prime spawning and nursery habitat.

Autumn steelhead of the Great Lakes have maintained this West Coast characteristic despite the shorter runs that are often typical of our smaller tributaries. Other theories, though, suggest that autumn runs may be nature's way of spreading risk among the entire population. This is said to ensure survival of the species.

My own personal theory is that autumn migration may be a life strategy steelhead use as a means of getting their eggs into the gravel prior to the appearance of the spring migrants which may greatly benefit their offspring.

Generally speaking, autumn run steelhead often enter streams with poorly developed gonads and are months away from spawning. They also appear to have a higher percentage of body fat upon river entry (Smith, 1968). Spring steelhead, on the other hand, enter rivers in closer proximity to the spawning period with well developed gonads.

Although both races spawn within the spring period it is the earlier running autumn race that seem to spawn weeks ahead of its spring spawning cohorts (personal observation).

➢ Homing and Migration ➢

Perhaps one of the most intriguing characteristics of a steelhead's life cycle is its uncanny ability to return to the same tributary in which it was spawned. Some scientific data supports that a steelhead can identify unique chemical compounds found in its natural stream at a rate of three parts per million to help guide it back home.

The most thorough study of homing done on steelhead was conducted by Shapovalov and Taft in 1954 on Waddell and Scott creeks, California. During this twelve-year study (1931-1942) 98.1% of the steelhead marked returned to Waddell Creek and of the Scott Creek study 97.1% returned (International North Pacific Fisheries Commission Bulletin 51).

Turning to the Great Lakes region, Jon George, Lake Superior steelhead biologist has also found very little evidence of straying throughout his Portage Creek study stream. Through tagging and annual assessments of life history characteristics, Jon and his dedicated crew of volunteers have estimated that a 1-2% stray rate for steelhead of the North (George and Bozel, 1994-2003 unpublished data).

However sophisticated a steelhead's sense of smell, there are additional environmental cues activating seasonal migrations. Data compiled at the Institute for Fisheries Research suggests that the beginning of the spawning run seems to be triggered by the photo period, or the shortening and lengthening of daylight in both spring and autumn. Though the most important cue may actually be temperature (Dodge and McCrimmon, 1970).

➢ Spawning Structure ➢

Great Lakes steelhead entering tributaries to spawn are comprised of varying year classes of mature adult fish. For the most part, the bulk of the spawning population is mainly maiden, or first time spawners (60-80%), as well as the less prominent, but equally important, repeat spawners (20-40%). Most maiden spawners enter the Great Lakes tributaries after their second year of lake growth and usually measure between 20-26 inches (50-65cm). Generally, they weigh from three to six pounds (1.3-2.7kg) although there are exceptions. Some steelhead will spend additional years feeding and growing in the lake prior to making their initial run upstream and enter the tributaries as true trophy-sized fish. As their name implies, repeat spawners have spawned at least once and have now embarked on their second, third or fourth jaunt to the spawning grounds. However, in many areas, they become less visible in the overall population. This is most likely a result of liberal fish limits and increased angler pressure.

Repeat spawning steelhead are an important component to the overall stream population of fish. According to Jon George, biologist with MNR and ardent steelheader, "Repeat spawners are your best spawners." They produce more and larger eggs and are able to construct redds in heavier currents over larger substrate and their fry also tend to be larger. Additionally, repeat spawners are able to produce greater numbers of offspring that can greatly contribute to the total population in years when maiden recruitment is low.

Generally speaking the population of maiden and repeat spawners varies somewhat across the Great Lakes. This is attributed to a broad spectrum of variables such as year-class strength, climate, geographic location and angling pressure.

According to David Swank (personal communication) who is doing his Ph.D. dissertation on life history variation in Great Lakes steelhead, if the repeat spawning population should sink to 30% this would be cause for concern especially if it were long term. According to Mr. Swank repeat spawning rates in wild Michigan steelhead populations are in the

Fisheries studies indicate that 98% of steelhead return to spawn in the river of their natural origins.

order of 30-60%. In Ontario's North Shore Lake Superior tributaries they prefer to see repeat rates of at least 50%.

The repeat spawning value was at one time very high along the North Shore of Lake Ontario. From 1971 to 1975 the repeat spawning index for female steelhead along the Ganaraska River was over 58%. From 1971 to 1975 the Ganaraska had one of the highest percentages of fish (12%) that had spawned three times (Biette and Dodge, 1981). The vast number of repeat spawners could be attributed to low angling pressure. In recent years, the repeat spawning population has been significantly reduced. The overall Ganaraska steelhead population has steadily declined in the last decade going from a peak run of 18,169 in 1989 to a dismal run of 3,500 fish in the spring of 2002.

It is estimated that the Ganaraska River should be capable of supporting an adult spawning population run of 10,000 fish (Jim Bowlby, personal communication). Biological data collected from the adult population indicates that overharvest may be the contributing factor to the low abundance of adults that currently exist. Liberal five-fish limits, climate change, fluctuating year classes, influx of anglers, and honed angler skills are all conspiring to disrupted the once plentiful resource offered on one of the most pristine rivers found along Lake Ontario's North Shore.

❖ Spawning and Rearing ❖

After easily negotiating instream obstructions during the increased river flows of spring, steelhead soon find themselves in prime spawning territory. Early migration constitutes first dibs over prime spawning riffles, however, there is generally enough gravel to be had by all. As females narrow down their nesting search large dark-colored males with protruding teeth and clamp-like jaws battle for the prospects of passing along their genetic lineage. Selecting a suitable site within a riffle with sufficient depth, velocity, and

Large spring males ready to pass on their genetic blueprints.

nearby cover, the female will slowly turn broadside and begin to displace fist-sized boulders, smaller rocks, and gravel by literally thrusting her body and tail as the dominant male keeps vigilant by her side while the eager subordinates try to manipulate him from his post.

Both males and females simultaneously quiver with open mouths as milt and eggs spill into newly formed nests. Moving slightly upstream the female constructs yet another nest that washes gravel over the recently deposited eggs, keeping well oxygenated water percolating throughout the bed. The whole process is repeated several times until the hen has deposited most, if not all, of her eggs. The act of spawning itself can be over within 12 hours, or can last several days, depending upon such variables as water temperature and increased stream flow after heavy periods of rain. Water temperatures during spawning normally range between 37°-49°F (3°-9.4°C) (Bell, 1973) but fish have also been observed in temperatures as low as 32.5°F (0.3°C) (Dodge and Macrimmon, 1971) and as high as 68°F (20°C) (Cederholm, 1984). Personally, the lowest I have observed spawning activity along a Lake Ontario tributary was at 36°F (2°C) while fish paired up at 33°F (.05°C). Ironically, not all steelhead migrate to upper river stretches to spawn. A small number of fish opt to spawn closer to the lakes. I have observed numerous generations of late winter steelhead spawning within a quarter mile of Lake Ontario in the first gravel riffle that is available.

❖ Spawning Over Pre-existing Redds ❖

Oddly enough, each season, steelhead spawn over the top of pre-existing spawning redds. Many anglers believe it is a result of a lack of sufficient spawning gravel. According to Chris Weland, graduate of the University of Guelph's Fisheries Science Program, this behavior may be the result of "imprinting." One of the spawning pair may have hatched out of that gravel section, or they may simply realize that the area has the most suitable gravel with the best flow and nursery habitat.

❖ Incubation and Emergence ❖

Percolating water within the gravel nest feeds life-sustaining oxygen to the newly deposited eggs while also flushing out carbon dioxide. Safely nestled within the redd, the eggs are four to six inches beneath the gravel and can number anywhere from 3,000 to 10,000 depending on the size and age of the hen that spawned them. One of the threats jeopardizing the survival of the incubating eggs is silt washes into the watershed from exposed and eroding hillsides after prolonged rain. Anglers also present a direct threat by wading through shallow riffles. Unlike the eggs of other trout and salmon species that over winter under the gravel, steelhead eggs are relatively quick to hatch, often hatching within four to six weeks of being fertilized. Temperature is said to be a governing factor in their development, the warmer the water temperature, the quicker they hatch. Prior to emergence, alevins (as they are now called), may spend an additional four to seven days under the gravel as they absorb the nutrients within their embryonic sacs while struggling to break free of the gravel.

➷ Fry Behavior Key ➹
to Long-term Survival

The tributaries of the Lower Great Lakes begin to see small numbers of newly emergent steelhead by early to mid-June. "Sac fry," as they are now termed, leave their gravel sanctuaries as one inch (2.5cm) juveniles and relocate along the shallow margins of stream banks where they absorb their remaining yolk sacs and start to take on the traditional coloration of a parr-marked rainbow. The earliest of emerging fry may very well be the offspring of autumn migrants that have spawned weeks in advance of the spring run. These offspring now have a one or two week growth and territory advantage over their later-hatching cohorts. (This may be another reason why autumn runs have adopted this life strategy.) With a 75-80% (Mackay) hatch rate spread over the remainder of June it doesn't take long for the expanding fry population to substantially increase. However, these increased numbers generally result in decreased feeding opportunities and as a consequence, territorial aggression spreads throughout the fry community.

It is obvious that the larger "first borns" grow quicker and overrule prime feeding lanes and in so doing displace smaller more submissive fry to the outer margins of the remaining habitat. Battles often ensue as first borns chase off smaller subordinate fry that try to enter their feeding space. It seems as though the first borns divide their time between feeding and chasing down defiant intruders. Displaced fry seem to cohabitate to a certain degree but, they too establish territories according to rank. The primary food source of these fry are minute emerging invertebrates that have to ride along the stream's surface film until they break free of their exoskeletons or nymphal shucks. Fry sit just under the surface to intercept them throughout this process.

Having invested significant time observing fry interactions, it becomes fairly apparent that the foundations to future survival and sustainability are already being built at this very early life stage. Dominant fish seem to possess the necessary life skills to carry them into the next life phase while those that lack the ability to adapt are weeded out through attrition. However, the playing field can become level and the losses heavy in the wake of a substantial rain event.

The Brule River system in Wisconsin is a prime example of the vulnerability that still exists for the entire fry population when mother nature deals them a losing hand. The decline of returning adults there caused great concern for fisheries officials. In their research, Pratt and Blust found that fry survival is conducive to stream flow. Heavy freshet, during the first two months after fry emergence, negatively impacts the new population of young fish. Heavy rains caused rivers to swell, and in the process, wash away the hatched fry. The rebound effect of such a catastrophic rain event on the young population was evident four years later as fewer fish survived to return as adults. This shows that although a large number of eggs may be deposited by the adults, in the end, it is the environment which ultimately decides if the year class survives or fails.

By late August extensive changes have taken place within the fry community. Fry have now grown to between 2-3 inches (6-8cm) and have vacated their early rearing habitat in favor of faster water, tailouts, and pools. No longer are they reliant upon tiny surface flies to fulfill their appetites, however, this isn't to say that should an opportunity present itself it wouldn't be taken advantage of. Quite simply the small surface-emerging invertebrates are less abundant at this time of year so a young steelhead orients its feeding activity towards mid-surface and bottom, utilizing the constant drift to supply its menu of plankton, larvae, ants, smaller terrestrials and infant

Upon emergence, fry locate along shallow stream margins. Here they set up and defend a territorial feeding lane.

stone and mayfly nymphs. It is interesting to note that these food items more than likely become imprinted onto a fish's memory as it grows, thus, upon its return as an adult, it may opportunistically feed on these same food items.

The overall fry population has also been visibly reduced by August. A 90% mortality rate is generally accepted as the norm. The high moralities are likely the result of limited food and space constraints. Overall, the population may also be reduced as not to exceed the carrying capacity of the river. Those that remain are now considered the new year-class by fisheries biologists.

The thinning of the year class population provides the survivors with better prospects of habitat selection and more profitable feeding opportunities. Also, having doubled in size since hatching, the young parr now have stronger swimming capabilities and are able to survive moderate variances in stream flow.

Heading into its first winter, the young parr, now 3-4 inches (6-8cm) long, will seek out refuge in the deeper confines of slower moving water and pools; the onset of winter presents new life challenges to the young parr who now face winter mortality. In his research paper on the effects of winter severity on steelhead smolts, Dr. Paul Seelbach of the Michigan Department of Natural Resources Institute for Fisheries, suggests that possible factors which cause over winter mortality in salmonid parr populations include hypothermia, inadequate lipid reserves, and subsequent starvation, predation, and physical damage from anchor and frazil ice.

Douglas Dodge, a former steelhead researcher with the Ontario Ministry of Natural Resources, states that the young of the year and yearling rely on fat reserves to see them through the winter and that very little feeding takes place (personal communication). Should the young fingerling steelhead survive until the following August, they will measure in at approximately 5-7 inches (12-17cm), and will over winter once, possibly twice more, before migrating to the big lake.

✢ Smolts ✢

It has been well documented that Great Lakes steelhead parr begin the physiological process of smolting anytime between the ages of one to three years. However, this is largely dependent on a number of variables such as geographic location, climate, body size and genetics.

Typically, lower Great Lakes wild populations seem to smolt out at age two while some populations within smaller Lake Superior tributaries have been known to adapt to a one year smolting history due to diminishing flows and droughts (Jon George, personal communication).

Scale samples taken from Great Lakes adult steelhead indicate that 10% emigrated at age one, 86% at age two, and 4% at age three (Dodge and MacCrimmon, 1970). Several Lake Superior populations have a dominance of one-year-old smolts that often exceed 80% of the adult population (George and Bozek, 1994 to 2003, unpublished data).

Smolting appears to have a genetic component rather than being size related (Sanders and Bailey 1976, and George and Bozek, 1994 to 2003, unpublished data). Due to a constant feeding regime hatchery raised fish can obtain smolt size much more quickly than fish born in the wild and can be stocked at age one. Stray rates are low for wild populations and high for stocked smolts indicating homing is developed from the egg stage and not during smolting. It seems that the same environmental cues that activate the upstream push of pre-spawn adults also influenced the emigration of the newly transforming smolt. Oddly enough the smolt population seems to emigrate in reverse chronological order as larger, three-year-old smolts descend first, followed by two-year-old smolts, then one-year-olds. Moving progressively downstream the Parr markings that have helped to conceal the juvenile since birth are now but a vague fading image as the smolt graduates towards the same chrome coloration representative of the adult population. Most smolt populations migrate from our Great Lakes tributaries at two years of age and in water temperatures between 48-63°F (9-17°C) two months after peak flow (Stauffer). According to Jim Bowlby of the Ministry of Natural Resources Lake Ontario Management Unit, as smolts leave, the unique scent and chemical compounds found within the watershed are imprinted on their memory. Smolts may also imprint on the scent emitted by the adult population as research indicates that this may be a character trait among Atlantic salmon. Jim Bowlby also explains that smolt emigration is prominent during the overnight periods as well as increased periods of flow and turbidity.

Yearling steelhead feed very little during winter and rely upon stored fat reserves to see them through.

Having volunteered with the O.M.N.R. while they conducted spring smolt enumerations, it was rather evident that the smolts favored emigration under the cover of darkness, especially when accompanied by the increased flows of late day showers. In all likelihood, night migration is a life strategy to help the young silvery smolts guard against larger predators such as bass, pike, birds of prey, raccoon and mink. (It appears that smolts are especially vulnerable in the last few slower flowing miles before the big lake.)

Research conducted on smolt activity along the steelheads native range of the Pacific Coast suggests that upon ocean entry, smolts move quickly offshore and experience rapid growth particularly in the first and second years of ocean life. This may also hold true for Great Lakes steelhead smolts as well. However, their quick dispersal into the vast forays of their new feeding grounds is short-lived as a fair portion of these one-lake-year steelhead will re-enter their native tributaries during September after only having spent one summer feeding and growing in the lake.

These "shakers," "skippers," or half pounders, as they are often referred to, have grown rapidly, already measuring in at 12-18 inches (30-45cm) and as their name implies, they weigh in at approximately 1/2 pound (.23kg). Just why these fish return after only spending four months in the open water is most likely a byproduct of their genetics. Perhaps these shakers are offspring of autumn migrants and are genetically programmed to run. Although most of these shakers are not sexually mature, some precocious males have been observed spawning with adult females. These same males are also the agitators that often infuriate adult males as they attempt to sneak in alongside the females during spawning.

One major myth about the early migration of shakers is that they are influenced to move upstream by the prospect of dining on free-drifting Chinook roe. While shakers will definitely take advantage of the free meal, I'm afraid they are only doing so opportunistically and not purposefully. (I site the greatest example of this behavior from Chris Atkinson, founder of the Nottawasaga Steelheaders. According to Chris, he caught more than his share of shakers from the Nottawasaga River prior to the presence of Chinook strays from Georgian Bay.)

➢ Smolt to Adult Survival ✦ Across the Great Lakes

As wild Great Lakes steelhead smolts move into their new open water environments they are further subjected to moralities that will reduce their overall returning populations. Smolt to adult survival around the Great Lakes is dependent upon a wide array of variables ranging from geographic location to seasonal climatic conditions, to size of smolt upon lake entry. It seems each lake, and its encompassing tributaries, has its own individual rate of smolt to adult survival. To simplify the smolt to adult survival percentages across the Great Lakes, Jon George, steelhead Biologist with the O.M.N.R. provided me with an insightful overview of smolt studies conducted throughout the last 30 years by various steelhead biologists from around the Great Lakes. The shores of Lake Superior seem to have the lowest wild smolt to adult survival rate ranging from 3% in some Minnesota streams, to 4.4% in Wisconsin's Pike Creek, and up to 6% survival for the Brule River system. These low survival rates exemplify the early emigration profile of some steelhead (parr) populations as they are forced out of their instream environments too early as a likely result of poor or decreasing instream habitats. Data compiled on Lake Michigan's Little Manistee River supports a 6% to 29% smolt to adult survival rate for smolts that have endured a two-year stream stay. The shifting survival margin is said to be the likely result of the onslaught of severe winters. Unlike the limited smolt to adult survival rate for some of the Lake Superior tributaries, and the fluctuating numbers of the Lake Michigan population, the Lake Huron/Ontario survival rate appears to index between 10% and 15%.

The disposition of a two- and sometimes three-year stream residency yields the Lake Huron/Ontario smolts a larger overall body size which seems to be paramount for smolt survival within the Great Lakes. Although the smolt to adult survival index contains numerical references and percentages, one must realize that many environmental variables exist that can easily cause fluctuations within each population.

Outgoing smolts are exposed to increases in predation during the last few slower flowing miles before the lake. This silvery smolt was attacked twice and escaped both times.

➢ Lake Residency ➣

Entering into the vast expanses of the Great Lakes provides smolts with greater opportunities for growth, but it also presents new challenges in terms of survival. Having spent from one to four years in their natural streams feeding on terrestrial insects, instream invertebrates, and even the odd fry from their own species, they now have a broader variety of food choices in their new Great Lakes environment. Smolt growth is rapid after entering the protein rich ecosystem as plankton and small baitfish are added to the daily menu of lake-wide invertebrates and terrestrials.

As steelhead continue to grow within the open pelagic water of the lake they are able to take in larger food items such as smaller alewives, smelt, perch and three spine sticklebacks. However, steelhead have been known to exhibit difficulties in chasing down larger baitfish. In fact M.N.R. records indicate that Lake Ontario steelhead consumed less than 2% of the total rainbow smelt population and were likely to consume a very small portion of the available alewife population.

To give further credence to a steelhead's inefficiency to capture faster moving prey fish within the Great Lakes, Savitz and Bardygula (1989) conducted a study to monitor interactions of Lake Michigan salmonids and their prey within the confines of a large aquarium. Their observations suggested that steelhead had a difficult time capturing prey in the open water and had to resort to trapping it in the corners or near the physical structures found within the aquarium. This is unlike Chinook and coho who seem to exhibit a more aggressive demeanor.

Since steelhead have a reduced capacity for capturing faster moving prey they have filled the void by consuming aquatic invertebrates and terrestrials found within the offshore scum lines where discarded debris and logs ride the discernible water slicks of intermixing lake temperatures. This is by no means a chore for the steelhead since they travel within the first 30-40 feet (9-12m) of the surface anyway.

Stomach analyses conducted in Lake Ontario by a charter boat friend of mine can further account for the consumption of terrestrials. Having dissected many steelhead, it was found that ladybugs make up a fair portion of a steelhead's stomach contents. In Lake Superior (Wisconsin), Sea Grant indicated that steelhead feed mostly on invertebrates (80%). However, Great Lakes steelhead are far from inept when it comes to foraging on certain segments of the baitfish population. Despite their relative lack of stealth in chasing down larger prey items, they have compensated by keying in on the younger segments of the alewife and smolt populations and by chasing slower moving baitfish such as three spine stickleback and perch.

Lake Michigan data indicates that yellow perch made up 58% (by weight) of prey consumed by one- and two-year-old steelhead and 17% of the diet of the three- and four-year-olds. It's interesting to note that the primary food source for steelhead in its ancestral waters of the Pacific Ocean consists of 63% shrimp, 31% squid, and of minor importance, amphipods (Mark Bere, D.F.O., personal communication).

Suffice it to say that the diversified food preferences of the Great Lakes steelhead is a big plus for the species as it would be voted most likely to survive in the event of prolonged baitfish decline.

➢ Age Classification, Life History ➣
and Adult Growth

To give structure to a steelhead population, fisheries managers have given age classifications for both the steelhead's instream juvenile residency and that of its adult life out in a Great Lake or the ocean. Once combined, these age structures formulate a life history which fisheries managers use to determine the average growth, age, and spawning characteristics within the total population. Therefore, a steelhead that exhibits a life history of 2/3 represents a fish that has spent two years as a juvenile in the stream environment and three years in the Great Lakes or ocean to give it a total age of five years. Several combinations of life histories exist throughout the Great Lakes depending upon genetics, as well as the period of time spent in stream or lake residencies. Much like rings on a tree, the growth patterns and life histories of a steelhead are transferred onto its scales which are examined by biologists to determine at what age it resided in its stream and lake environments and to see how many times it has spawned. Through scale analysis, biologists have concluded that steelhead growth is not determined by age but is rather determined by the amount of time spent feeding in the protein rich environment of either lake or ocean. Age at first maturity may also affect growth potential.

In his book *The Steelhead Trout* by Trey Combs (Frank Amato Publications), Combs often refers to some important biological data that was complied on the life histories of the steelhead in Waddell Creek in California. The study, conducted by Leo Shapovolov and Alan C. Taft, indicated that fish of equal age can demonstrate variable growth rates as determined by their stream or lake environments. The study indicated that a fish of exactly the same age, but with different life histories, show a vast difference in their growth and weight.

Let's take a closer look; a steelhead with a 3/1 (stream/ocean) life history weighed in at just over three pounds where as the opposite life history of the same age 1/3 (ocean/stream) resulted in a much larger fish of 12 pounds (5.4kg). The ages were exactly the same, however, the steelhead that spent three years in the ocean, instead of in the stream, grew to be the larger fish.

Generally speaking, most Great Lakes steelhead adhere to a 2/2 (stream/lake) life history and return as four-year-old maiden spawners. Fish returning to Lake Ontario and Georgian Bay tributaries as maidens are generally 20-26 inches (50-65cm) in length and can weigh in at 3-6.6 pounds (1.5-3 kg). (Chris Atkinson, personal communication.) While the Lake Superior population only seems to measure in at around 17-21 inches (45-55 cm), and weighing 2-4 pounds (0.9-1.8kg) due to colder climatic conditions and poorer nutrient capacities (Jon George, personal communication).

The tape measure on the next page shows the potential length at each age for Lake Superior steelhead. Keep in mind that steelhead of the lower Great Lakes can express greater growth rates at first and subsequent spawning. This is due to warmer climates and increased nutrient capacities within the lower lakes.

→ Large-Growth Strategies ←

Since we now have a somewhat better understanding of how a steelhead's life history is broken down i.e.: stream years verses lake years and number of times having spawned, let's now take a look at how all this adds up in terms of steelhead growth and what variables exist for producing those true Great Lakes giants.

We have already touched upon the maiden spawning population throughout this chapter but there is a small segment of this population that we have yet to discuss. Although most maiden spawners generally fall into the three to six pounds (1.3-2.7kg) category, there are those in this population that refuse to be labeled quite so easily. Some Great Lakes steelhead making their maiden spawning migration may exceed weights of 20+ pounds (9kg). These rare individuals (less than 1% of the population) have been genetically programmed for fast growth, late maturity, and longevity.

Steelhead of this magnitude are important spawners in wild populations. It seems the larger males are

On his Portage Creek study stream, Lake Superior steelhead biologist Jon George has been tagging and observing the life history characteristics of steelhead in one of their most remote northerly Great Lakes locations. His tagging and research program focuses on repeat spawners and maiden recruitment.

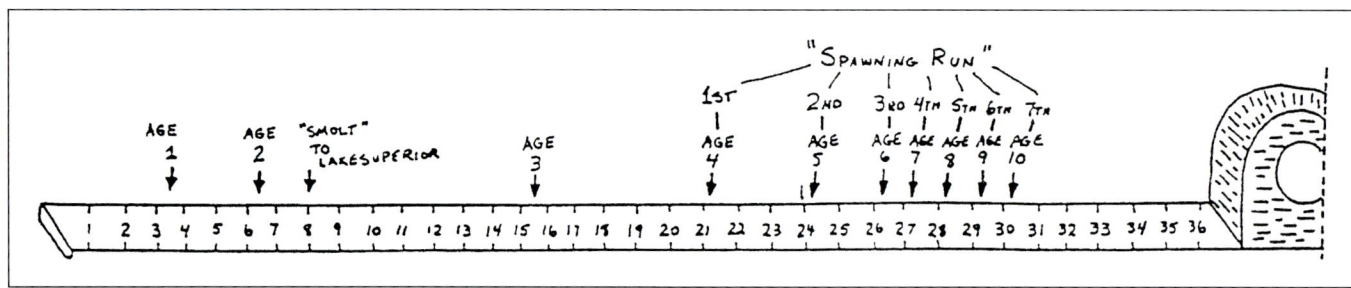

Age classification, life history and adult growth.

of greater value than larger females merely because they have the capacity to spawn multiple times within a given spawning year. These overgrown steelhead, typically of the lower Great Lakes, have attained their "trophy status" and large growth capacities by having spent consecutive, uninterrupted years feeding and growing within the rich forage base lakes without having taken any time off for spawning as opposed to having lived the traditional life history of making consecutive annual spawning runs. However, the large growth capacity of steelhead isn't only limited to that minute segment of the maiden spawning population, it seems to be more prevalent among repeat spawners, although repeat spawners seem to take greater amounts of time achieving trophy status due to the fact that their time dedicated to spawning is lost as a growth period.

Generally speaking, most adult steelhead can lose up to one-third of their body weight during upstream spawning migrations. Under this regime, a steelhead first has to regain its lost weight, and replenish its gonads prior to making any gains in total body weight therefore overall growth is greatly reduced. Steelhead that survive to repeat spawn for the fourth and fifth times can become large fish but the chances of a steelhead surviving to spawn beyond a third time are very slim, especially if harvest is high.

Although steelhead growth is primarily a function of its own genetics and lake residency, there are other contributing factors which ultimately lead to its overall growth—that being a protein-rich forage base and the extent of its annual growing season. An early spring and a late winter provide steelhead with added opportunities for growth. The growing season can be further extended should steelhead decide to take up residence off the warm water discharges of Great Lakes' power-generating stations throughout the winter period.

Generally speaking, Great Lakes steelhead that attain weights of greater than 20 pounds (9kg) probably contain the genetics for late maturity and longevity. It probably also lives in an environment which promotes an extended growing season with an ample food supply. In Lake Superior tributaries the largest steelhead seemed to have obtained their large sizes by having three or four lake years prior to maturity. (George & Bozek, 1994-2003, unpublished data.)

Giant Great Lakes steelhead are rare gems that make up the smallest portion of any given steelhead population. In essence, they may number less than 1% of a total population. In order to grow fish to the 20 pound (9kg) plus category, steelhead have to survive to at least five or six years and beyond which is rare in itself. Despite their low densities, these behemoth steelhead do manage to sink the floats of some fortunate steelheaders each season as

Large steelhead achieve true trophy status as a result of genetics and varying life history characteristics. Some maiden spawners spend additional years growing in the lake prior to their first spawning run and grow to trophy sizes. Repeat spawners may take more time to reach trophy status because the time they dedicated to spawning is lost as a growth period. Repeats first have to regain lost weight and replace gonads prior to any weight gains. Where fish located throughout winter may also increase their growth potential.

word of their capture quickly spreads throughout local angling communities.

So how large can some Great Lakes steelhead become? According to various Great Lakes fisheries statistics most record steelhead have all weighed in at over 20 pounds (9kg). Below is a list of record steelhead caught from across the Great Lakes:

Location	Weight	Year
Lake Ontario (NY)	26.15lbs/11.8kg	1985
Lake Erie	20.97lbs/9.0kg	1997
Lake Huron/ Georgian Bay	29.02lbs/13.15kg	1975
Lake Michigan	27.02lbs/12.2kg	1987
Lake Superior	17.06lbs/7.8kg	1980

The largest steelhead was taken in 1975 from Georgian Bay at 29.02 pounds (13.15kg). Douglas Dodge, a retired Great Lakes steelhead biologist, informed me that back in 1968 he boated a 31 pound (14kg) steelhead from Lake Huron while conducting a survey. The fish obviously did not qualify for any sort of record because it was caught in a sampling net, though it does however exemplify the large growth potential of some of our Great Lakes steelhead.

Generally speaking, most Great Lakes regions have the potential to produce steelhead over and above the 20 pound (9kg) plus category but, in order to connect with one of these rare individuals your timing must be right as these colossal giants seem to adhere to an elusive regime. (We will explore the prospects of connecting with these Great Lakes treasures a little later in the autumn and winter steelhead sections.)

✈ Swimming Speeds ✦ and Distances Traveled

Steelhead, whether from their ancestral watersheds of the Pacific Ocean, or their introduced species of the Great Lakes are known for travelling great distances throughout their lifetimes. In some cases, Great Lakes steelhead have been known to travel outside of their natal home lakes and enter upon distant Great Lakes not of their initial origin. Steelhead stocked in Lake Erie often end up in Lake Ontario. Lake Michigan fish often transverse into the tributaries of Georgian Bay. A case in point takes me back many years ago to the Nottawasaga River, a tributary of Georgian Bay. After landing a fresh autumn steelhead, a fishing aquaitance realized that his steelhead was missing a unique combination of fins. After inquiring about the steelheads's origins, it was determined that the fish had its humble beginnings in Lake Michigan.

For the most part steelhead return to their natal rivers but within some populations there is a genetic predisposition which suggests that a steelhead will stray from its home watershed. Out-planted hatchery raised smolts seem to stray more than wild fish as a likely result of not having properly imprinted the watershed after relaese.

In terms of swimming speeds and distances traveled, steelhead have been probed, tagged, and fitted with transmitters all in the good name of science. The accumulated data has provided insightful knowledge as to the migratory behaviors of steelhead throughout all aspects of their ocean, lake and stream residencies.

Swimming speeds, for instance, have been divided into three categories: cruising speeds, sustained speeds, and burst speeds. Cruising speeds can be endured for great lengths of time and are primarily used for long distance travel. Sustained speeds are used to negotiate rapids, flats, and difficult passages. Burst speeds are primarily used for feeding and escaping but are often of very short duration.

Generally speaking, cruising speeds equate to 4.6 feet per second (or 1.40m/sec), sustained speeds reach 13.7 feet per second (or 4.18m/sec), and burst speeds can reach 26.5 feet per second (or 8.08m/sec) (B Jornn and Reiser, 1991).

Data from the International North Pacific Fisheries Commission (Bulletin Number 51) indicates that steelhead tagged offshore and then recovered in spawning streams provide the best rates of movement for steelhead. Of the 78 fish tagged offshore, 13 were recovered within the given research time allotted. The average distance traveled for those fish was 31 miles (50km) per day. The fastest fish swam a distance of approximately 894 miles (1.438km) in just 17 days at a rate of 53 miles (85km) per day. The slowest fish took 50 days to travel 474 miles (762km) at a rate of 9.4 miles (15.2km) per day.

Similar tagging surveys have also taken place on the Skeena River system—home to some of the largest steelhead in the world. One tagged Skeena steelhead was known to have traveled upstream nearly 90 miles (144km) in two days, while the average daily upstream movement of 95 tagged fish was about 5 miles (8km). If fish can migrate upstream against currents with such relative speed, imagine how fast they can head downstream after their spawning duties are completed.

One North Umpqua study suggests that a post-spawn steelhead traveled 25 miles in only 27 hours (Salmon Trout Steelheader, Aug/Sept 2000). Suffice it to say that steelhead are capable of swimming great distances in short time frames, however, the distances traveled throughout a watershed depend upon many things such as stream height, flow and water temperatures.

Autumn migrating steelhead of the Great Lakes generally migrate during summer low-water regimes, and while some are seemingly determined to crash through the shallows, they are often deterred from further migration due to impossible natural obstructions in the form of beaver dams and log jams. On the contrary high water promotes greater traveling distances in shorter time frames, this happens especially just before the spring spawn.

❖ Feeding and Migration ❖

Migrating back into their respective rivers after foraging and growing in their Great Lakes environment, adult steelhead are easily caught by seasoned anglers on suggestive, impressionistic, and realistic baits that resemble the basic menu of their juvenile instream residency. However, the greatest paradox concerning fish behavior is whether or not steelhead are actually feeding during their river migrations. The subject of instream feeding behavior is full of controversy and conjecture, much of which has sparked some debate among veteran steelheaders. It would be easy to formulate an opinion judging by our successes, obviously if we are catching fish then they must be hungry, therefore, they are on the feed. However simplistic this may appear, there really is much more to so-called feeding than meets the proverbial eye.

Examining stomach samples—whether through dissection of a kept fish or by means of a stomach pump—one soon discovers that a steelhead's stomach is usually void of any food items on most accounts, hence the paradox. So why then are fish willing to take our presentations if they don't seem to be feeding? There are a number of hypothetical answers to this question, all of which have merit.

One answer could very well be attributed to conditioning. Steelhead may be simply reacting to drifting baits with a trained response relating back to its juvenile behavior when it once had to compete and defend territory. Perhaps these trained responses continued into adulthood. Regardless of whether or not they require food once they are grouped together within the confines of a pool or run, they may compete for a drifting morsel such as they did when they were grouped as newborns and parr. James Bowlby, a biologist with the Lake Ontario Management Unit, suggests that steelhead, for the most part, aren't really feeding, but are acting more out of a reflex than anything else (personal communication).

One study done in British Columbia suggests that it may not be necessary for steelhead to feed once in the river system. This conclusion was drawn after some adult summer steelhead were held captive in a hatchery without being fed for 11 months prior to spawning with no apparent ill effects!

On the contrary, there are occasions that we do in fact find evidence of feeding behavior. On some occasions throughout the angling season, we have found *Hexagenia Limbata* nymphs jam packed in our steelhead stomach samples. These burrowing mayfly nymphs occupy the silty stream bottoms of the lower river sections where steelhead often stage. Finding these 1 1/2 inch (3.8cm) long nymphs in stomach samples should reveal a timeline of river travel if fish are kept within the upstream river sections. Other food items found include tiny backswimmers, eggs, small worms, midges and partially digested nymphs. Some anglers claim to have found tiny crayfish, not to mention some undigestables such as cigarette butts and bottle caps. (Ironically, I have yet to find evidence of any type of stream-dwelling minnows during any searches which may give credence to the Savitz and Barygula study which suggested that steelhead showed difficulty capturing prey fish when they conducted their tank study.)

Once steelhead enter migration mode they seem to feed more out of opportunity rather than necessity. Stomach samples may simply reflect sparse feeding opportunities, and as such anglers may be connecting with fish simply because they have presented the only feeding opportunity that the steelhead has encountered. To throw a further complication into the mix, steelhead may switch from opportunistic feeding, in favor of selective feeding, leading steelheaders to believe that the fish have moved out. (Selective feeding can occur as a result of angling pressure and the availability of food sources conducive to seasonal changes.)

To answer the question as to whether or not steelhead are actively feeding during their upstream migrations my answer would have to be both yes and no. Suffice it to say that adult steelhead maximize their feeding and growth potential out in the lake or ocean as a means of supporting their upstream migration. Streams, therefore, are used simply as wintering areas prior to spawning, and should steelhead encounter food along the way, it can merely be considered a territorial, competitive, or opportunistic snack.

Hexagenia *(burrowing mayfly) nymphs are often found in the stomachs of steelhead holding in lower slow flowing pools and estuary water. Most stomach samples usually show up empty. The question whether or not steelhead are actively feeding can not be answered with a yes or no. Fish may be taking drifted baits out of instinctive reflex actions or as a result of opportunity.*

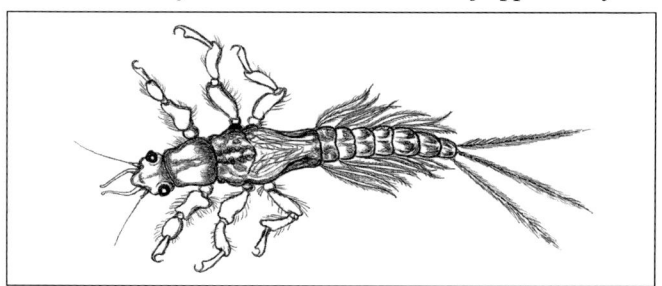

Chapter 2
Steelhead Water

Perhaps one of the greatest goals that a steelheader can achieve is obtaining an intimate working knowledge of the rivers he frequents.

Steelhead rivers—both large and small—seem to adhere to a regime of pools, riffles, runs, and flats, and they generally meander through valleys until reaching their final destinations.

These physical features are found within all watersheds and are primarily developed by two principal forces. These forces are gravity and friction. As water moves downstream (gravity) it slows and bounces (friction) off instream obstructions such as boulders, rocks, fallen trees, and the riverbank itself. This, of course, carves out pools, riffles and runs which steelhead utilize for holding, migration, and spawning. It is the peak discharge in spring though that forms the actual river features and the base flow that maintains them.

As a river flows downstream it generally does so with side-to-side and lateral movements which shift from one side of the river to the other. This is visually apparent at most river bends or meanders as the main current (thalweg) can be seen crossing over to the opposite shore. (This stream feature can also be identified by the floating bubbles, twigs and leaves that ride on its surface.)

Generally speaking, the deepest water will occur at most river bends (pools) where the thalweg rides along the stream bank. The lateral movement of water within the pool (transverse flow) picks up and redeposits fine sands, gravel, and leaves onto the opposite shore forming a point bar. This point bar is often what we anglers are standing on while float fishing a pool.

As the river progresses downstream from the pool, and proceeds to cross over, there is a rising in the riverbed and an increase in flow. This is generally referred to as a riffle, and in some instances, a flat.

Within the riffle, pool, run regime lies a host of additional steelhead waters which fish utilize as migrating and holding areas throughout different seasons, conditions, and water temperatures. Once water temperatures become suitable for steelhead the window of opportunity opens and steelhead migration can occur at just about any time during autumn, winter, or spring.

Making the transition from its large lake hunting grounds back to its comparable smallish river of natal origins must be met with some uncertainty by steelhead. The river environment—with its myriad of shallow flats, riffles, and obstructions—is quite unlike the deep-water sanctuary that lakes provide. However, the urge to migrate and spawn appears stronger than a fish's apprehensions so it proceeds upstream with both vigor and discretion. Those which the urge seems strongest in are willing to migrate during low flows under the cover of darkness, while those less willing seem to await the arrival of rainfall or snow melt (freshets) making for a more concealed migration. However, keep in mind that larger flowing rivers, with their abundant holding water and flow, tend to attract earlier migrations. Smaller flows, with their deep-water sanctuaries just upstream from a Great Lake, also attract early upstream movement that generally stalls at the first shallow water area. Fish here tend to sporadically proceed upstream under the cloak of darkness during the early morning and evening periods. This scenario will become redundant as steelhead move upstream during periods of low light then hold throughout the majority of the day. Typically, this also holds true for the upstream areas of larger flowing streams, as well until a freshet levels the playing field and allows for easier all-around access.

Therefore, in order to determine what physical areas of a river fish will utilize one must first assess the current river conditions. Once the general river and migratory assessment are made, then the entire watershed can be broken down into smaller increments conducive to steelhead utilization. Understanding the basic areas of a river that steelhead will inhabit during the different phases of migration is a skill that can be easily learned in time without much hardship. For the novice, books and periodicals provide a great general starting reference however, your real education will come when you combine armchair reading with on stream experience.

One of the quickest ways to identify potential holding water is to first eliminate all of the non-productive water that surrounds it.

Generally speaking, shallow water is of little value to a migrating steelhead already in a low-water environment as is deep water during periods of increased flows and swollen streams. So what then constitutes potential holding water? Where will a steelhead choose to locate? To answer this we must first look at a steelhead's basic instream requirements. A steelhead chooses a location, or holdover area, for several reasons: comfort, security, and to a lesser extent, but also worthy of note, opportunity. However, should one of these primary prerequisites become compromised either due to angling pressure or other stresses then the steelhead will hastily relocate until they have once again found comfort and security.

Therefore, the most productive steelhead waters during normal stream flows are mostly found within pools and runs followed by pockets, seams and riffles.

✦ Pools ✦

Pools generally form at river bends and are of primary importance because they offer steelhead the greatest amount of comfort and security. Another

Autumn Locations: Once autumn water temperatures drop to between 54-39° F (12-4°) expect fish to suspend throughout the tailout, the deep channel, the top of pool areas, (head) behind boulders and throughout runs. Fish tailouts first in autumn as fish will situate here after having run through the shallow flat. In faster flowing rivers fish the slower currents along the inside seam.

Winter Locations: Winter fish in 32-35° F (0-2° C) water temperatures will always locate near the bottom so fish deep. Look for fish within the slowest flows throughout the deep run, channel and under cut bank. The deep pool and back eddy are classic wintering areas.

Early Spring Pre Spawn: Early spring water temperatures in the 32-39°F (0-4°C) range see fish alternating between migrating and holding. This is dependent upon shifting weather scenarios. In stable or warming weather fish will rest behind boulders, around the head of the pool and in the run above the pool. Watch for wakes as new fish enter the area from downstream. With the return of cold weather, expect fish to relocate back to wintering areas.

Late Spring Post Spawn: Fish suspend off bottom once again as water temperatures increase to the 39-63 °F (4-17° C) range. Look for fish in pools, around blowdowns, runs and seams. In faster flowing areas such as deeper riffles and rapids, fish will locate closer to bottom. Fish will also chose to locate in front of and behind large stream boulders.

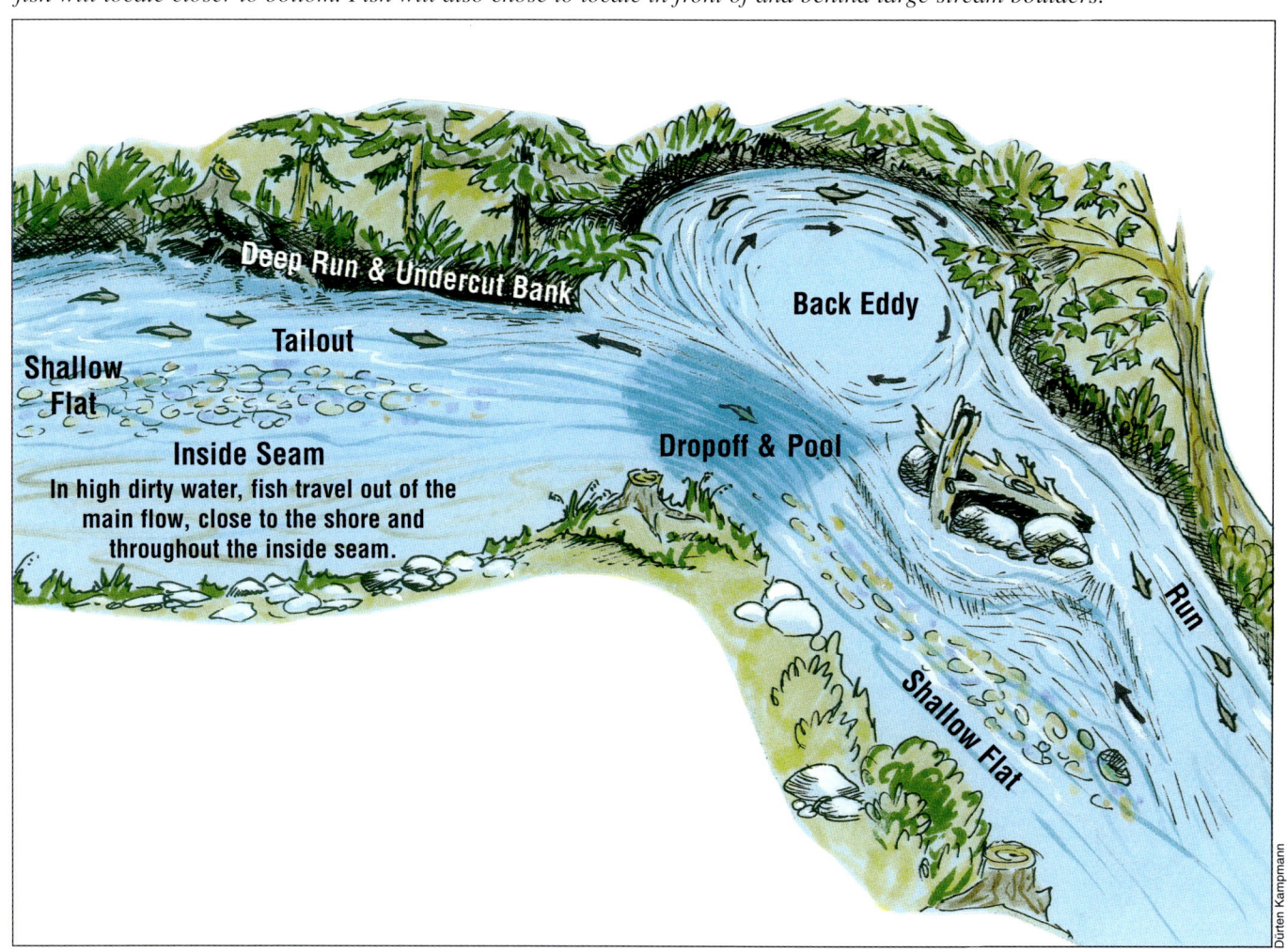

great pool feature is undercut banks which may form along the bend of a pool. There, steelhead are protected on three sides of their body: above, beneath, and along one of their sides. (Undercuts also make great ambush points for opportunistic steelhead.) In some pool situations back eddies are present and easily identified as areas of reverse flows adjacent to the main flow. Steelhead love back eddies because of their depth and the slower reversing flows which often trap food items. This creates greater feeding opportunities.

It is important to realize that steelhead which locate within a back eddy will be facing into the current and not necessarily upstream. Locating steelhead in pools without the added features of an undercut bank or a back eddy seems relatively simple. Steelhead will generally locate at the head (top), mid-section (middle) or the tailout (bottom end) of the pool but, all is not as simple as it may first seem since steelhead will locate at different sections within the pool environment according to migration phase, as well as varying water depths and temperature.

In upcoming chapters on seasonal steelhead we will go into greater detail on the aspects of steelhead behavior within the pool environment in relation to migration and temperature. We will also discuss baits and techniques that will constantly put you in the strike zone and into more fish.

↣ Runs ↢

Aside from pools and other areas of deep water, runs seem to be the next favorite locale among steelhead. Runs are areas generally over knee deep and can be found in-between pools and riffles. They mostly occur alongside riverbanks or bends and are generally used as holdover areas during migration. The flow throughout a run can also be greater than that of a pool.

↣ Riffles ↢

Riffles are areas of swiftly flowing shallow water which contain coarse rubble, gravel, stones, and rocks. They may indeed be considered the lifeblood of any steelhead stream for it is within these highly oxygenated flows that many aquatic life forms and food chains begin. Not only do future generations of steelhead hatch from riffles, but many populations of aquatic invertebrates also colonize here, in turn, providing occasional feeding opportunities for observant yearlings situated nearby.

In short, ample feeding opportunities exist throughout pools in close proximity to riffles areas, especially during spawning season when large adult females tear up the gravel and shake loose clinging nymphs from the underside of rocks. This provides all facets of the steelhead population with a smorgasbord of free-drifting inverts not to mention a copious supply of loose drifting roe. As already

Seam areas occur where fast, moderate and slow water areas converge. Seams also occur around instream obstructions such as fallen trees, logs, boulders or chunks of fallen stream banks. Generally seams occur naturally at riverbends or when instream obstructions fall into the stream at varying angles.

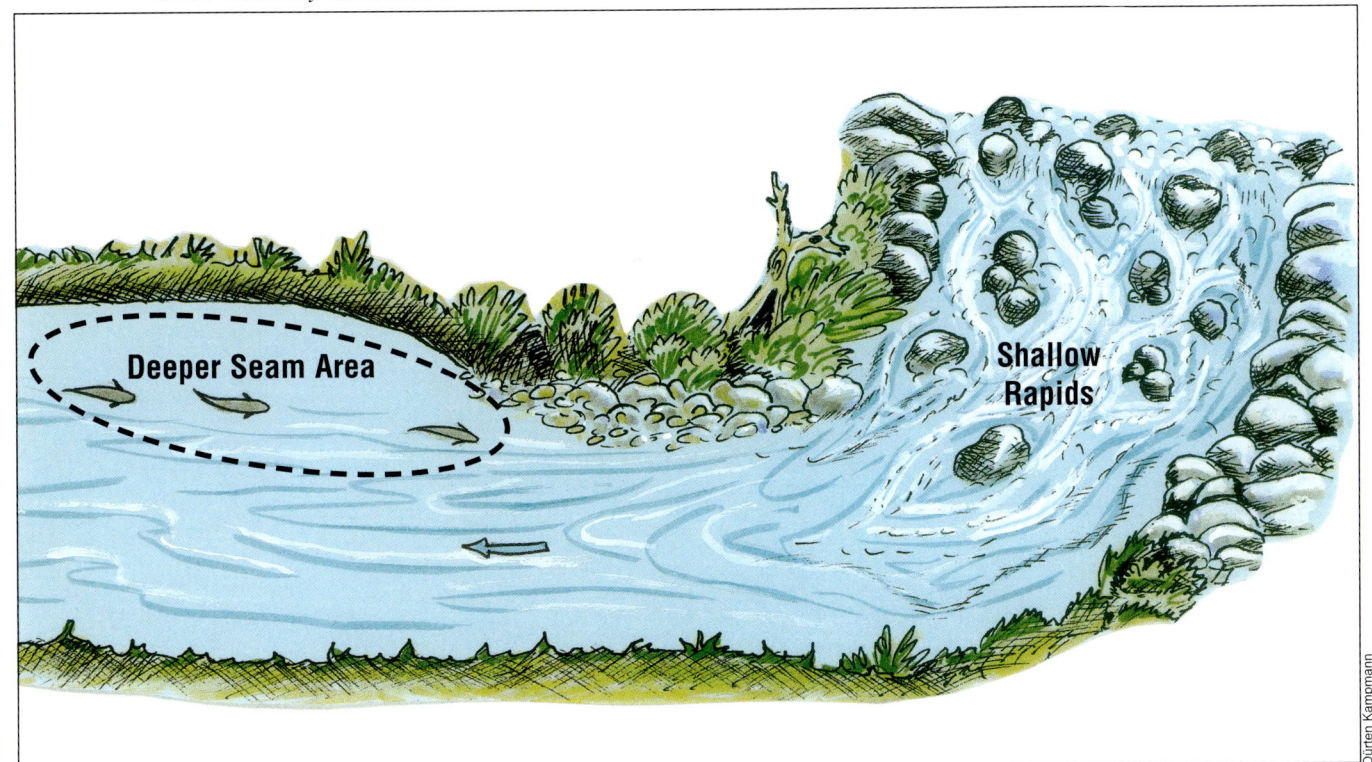

CHAPTER 2: STEELHEAD WATER | 21

cited, fast flowing riffle areas are used by adult steelhead for the purpose of spawning and at no other time throughout their life are steelhead more vulnerable. It is also at this time that steelheaders need to exercise a sincere respect for the resource and allow the spawning pair to proceed uninterrupted.

⇸ Deep Riffles and Rapids ⇷

During periods of prolonged angling pressure drop back steelhead may become stressed enough to vacate a clear, slow-flowing pool in favor of faster flowing water. Due to the stress factor, steelies may relocate to deeper, faster-flowing riffle or rapids—generally less than knee deep.

These areas are quite often overlooked by hasty anglers in a rush to fish more likely holding water. Generally, anglers end up walking right past good numbers of steelhead sitting in the deep riffles hidden by broken water overhead. This behavior is common on both large and mid-sized streams and rivers.

⇸ Pocket Water ⇷

Located within faster flowing sections, pockets are small holding spaces found alongside current breaks or swifter water. Watch for pocket water to form around rock outcrops and fallen timber.

⇸ Seams ⇷

Seams are one of my favorite places to drift a float. Relatively speaking seams can be defined as areas within the flow where slow and swifter currents converge. They are easily recognizable since the intermixing currents generally flow alongside, and downstream, of instream obstructions. Downed trees, boulders, large logs, and fallen chunks of stream bank that protrude into the water and alter the flow will likely have seam water around them. Seams also form at varying streambed elevations found within a stream stretch. Perhaps the best seam locations occur at swift river bends. Seams appeal to steelhead because they can rest within the edge of the current as well as optimize any feeding opportunities that may drift by.

⇸ Flats ⇷

Flats are seldom used by steelhead in slow to moderately flowing rivers. However, they are important to the steelheader because shallow flats often discourage migration, forcing most steelhead to gather in holdover pools awaiting more favorable water conditions. The brave few that do choose to chance the shallow flats always get my complete attention mostly for the sheer enjoyment of watching them negotiate the challenge. Generally speaking, fish chance the flats throughout the evening hours, and during the low-light periods of dusk and dawn, coming to rest in holdover pools throughout the day. But don't forget that fish may choose to rest in shallow featureless flats after a freshet has discolored the water during migration.

⇸ Boulders and Blowdowns ⇷

Both boulders and blowdowns play an integral part in determining steelhead location as we have been mentioning throughout this section, however, they deserve to be broken down into individual holding structures. Large boulders can become steelhead magnets simply because of the current breaks they provide. (Not only are they used by the adult migratory population, but they're also used by the young of the year and yearlings. Remember, everything a steelhead learns as a juvenile is re-applied during its return as an adult.) Depending upon its configuration, large boulders can provide a hydraulic escape for fish on the move. Contrary to popular belief steelies will rest directly in front of a large boulder amidst what appears to be a strong current when in

Blowdowns (fallen trees) offer steelhead added comfort and security. When blowdowns fall parallel to riverbanks throughout deeper pools or runs they become steelhead magnets

reality the current is divided and reduced as it works its way around the obstruction. Steelies will also rest behind the boulder, riding the upstream vortex as water reverses its flow and decelerates.

Blowdowns, or fallen trees, also hold their fare share of fish, especially during low flows. Should you be fortunate enough to locate one that has fallen parallel to a riffle/pool combination you will have the added advantage of broken water, all of which provides the steelie with comfort and security.

✣ Additional Steelhead Water ✤

Aside from the waters previously discussed, there is additional steelhead water that isn't as easily definable. The lower stretches of some streams which I fish are slow moving, deep-water areas that meander through marshland until reaching the water of a big lake. These lower sections are neither pools nor runs but are more reminiscent of a deep-water trench with its only features being its meandering, its depth, and the occasional blowdown. I must also add that during certain times of the year large numbers of steelhead will stack up in these lower river sections prior to migration.

✣ Annual Changes ✤

Despite a river's general flow regime and stable summertime characteristics, changes often lurk during periods of peak discharge. Ice jams and peak spring flows contain enough energy to relocate rather large boulders and topple trees from eroded streambanks. Watch for the creation of new holding water such as pools, runs and pockets as the stream redefines its flow around these obstructions. Keep in mind that the varying flows may also have a negative impact on pre-existing holding water as they may be subjected to silt deposits which will slowly start to fill the area in. Over time, blowdowns have the potential to turn into log jams which are bad news as they often obstruct steelhead migrations moving up or downstream. I encourage all steelheaders to take time out of their busy angling days to help clear access routes so that steelies may get to their intended destinations.

Chapter 3
Subtle Presentations

❥ Fishing with Floats ❦

How many times have you heard it? You know, that whipping sound that slashes through the cold morning air followed by the proverbial, "Fish on!" You glance over to see what the other guy is using and if you are fishing a Great Lakes tributary, nine times out of ten, the person fighting that scrappy robust steelhead has their bait suspended underneath a sensitive float of one shape or another.

As float fishing for Great Lakes steelhead becomes increasingly more popular and new and improved equipment becomes available, it is interesting to note that of all the specialized float fishing equipment—from long limber noodle rods to free spooling float reels—it is the inexpensive float that is our most productive piece of equipment.

Often colorful, floats are the tools which our presentations are based upon. They offer us controlled depth fishing, keep our baits suspended off snag infested bottoms, they signal subtle and aggressive takes from often moody steelhead, they allow us to present our offerings in a free drifting natural manner, not to mention they can also be used to establish pool depth which is paramount to our cold water success.

Although we may subconsciously pay attention to rod positioning and line placement while working

Suspending baits beneath our sensitive floats is one of the most efficient methods to deliver a free drifting natural presentation. Here the author displays the rewards of a properly executed float presentation.

a drift, it is really the inexpensive float that captivates and holds our immediate attention. Half the fun of float fishing is watching and waiting in eager anticipation for the float to register a hit or strike from a wary steelhead who was fooled by your properly presented bait. Seeing the distinctive hit or that subtle tap, tap, which leaves you wondering just when to set the hook is the pinnacle of any float fisherman's time on the water. For me, it is the most intriguing element of steelheading. It is a sheer and instant overdose of adrenaline that leaves me always wanting more.

Now that we know what floats can do to our central nervous system, let's get a little more technical and explore them in greater detail.

Rebounding steelhead populations during the 1960s began to spark intrigue among the Great Lakes angling community and by the 1970s refinements in terminal tackle and angling techniques began to emerge. Prior to the first introduction of steelhead floats it seems that bottom bouncing baits through the faster flows was the most prominent angling method used to connect with a Great Lakes steelhead. However, the introduction and effectiveness of suspending baits beneath floats to unsuspecting steelhead saw anglers trading in their bottom bouncing gear in favor of these colorful lightweight cork, balsa and Styrofoam tools.

Nearly three decades ago, float selection for Great Lakes steelhead was rather sparse. Since the concept of float fishing was still relatively new to Great Lakes anglers, some research, development, and innovation began to take place. Great Lakes steelheaders opted to embark on a crusade that would lead them to more sophisticated float shapes and designs to best suit their stream fishing needs.

To fill the void, anglers began to search elsewhere for concepts and designs. Looking West, British Colombian floats were decidedly too large for Great Lakes tributaries and soon Great Lakes anglers began adopting floats from the United Kingdom. Anglers from the U.K. were the virtual pioneers of float size, shape, and function and by adopting some of their styles, along with some local styles that began to emerge, Great Lakes steelheaders soon had a broad base of floats from which to choose from. Today Great Lakes anglers have narrowed down their stream float selections to four or five different styles amidst a broad selection of various sizes. Some styles have specific applications, while others are used throughout a variety of waters.

Generally speaking, Great Lakes float shapes are divided into four categories: those used for fast water, those for slow and moderate flows, those used for windy applications, and those used for deep water. Float size is also considered to be dependent upon additional factors such as distance to holding water, wind direction, current speed, and feeding behavior.

✦ Float Types and Shapes ✦

Float shapes are designed to efficiently ride the various currents found within the stream environment while at the same time offering the least amount of resistance to unsuspecting fish on the bite. Therefore, one should try to match float shape to current speed.

Floats for faster flowing regions of the Great Lakes include the grayling or inverted tear drop, the round quill, and the short stout elongated chubber. These bulkier float shapes allow for increased shot capacities which are needed to get baits down quicker within the faster flows.

Floats designed for slow to moderate currents are somewhat longer in size and tend to be more slender in shape. These styles include the avon, porcupine quill, and the pencil variety. Their long slender shapes make efficient use of slow to moderate flows and easily detect subtle takes from shy biting steelhead.

Given the above descriptions, one must realize that a whole slew of hybrid float shapes exists contrary to the basic designs already mentioned. Some float shapes have been combined to match multiple

Various float shapes and sizes were designed to efficiently ride through particular currents. Some shapes can be used for both slow and fast water applications. In the end the ultimate decision on float use boils down to personal preference. From top to bottom: For fast water use, inverted Graylings are a popular choice. For medium flows, Avon's often work well. Slow flows call for slender types of floats such as the pencil or porcupine quill. Bothersome downstream winds call for Wagglers. For deep water fishing slip floats are best. Left: A plumb bomb is the simplest way to accurately determine pool depths.

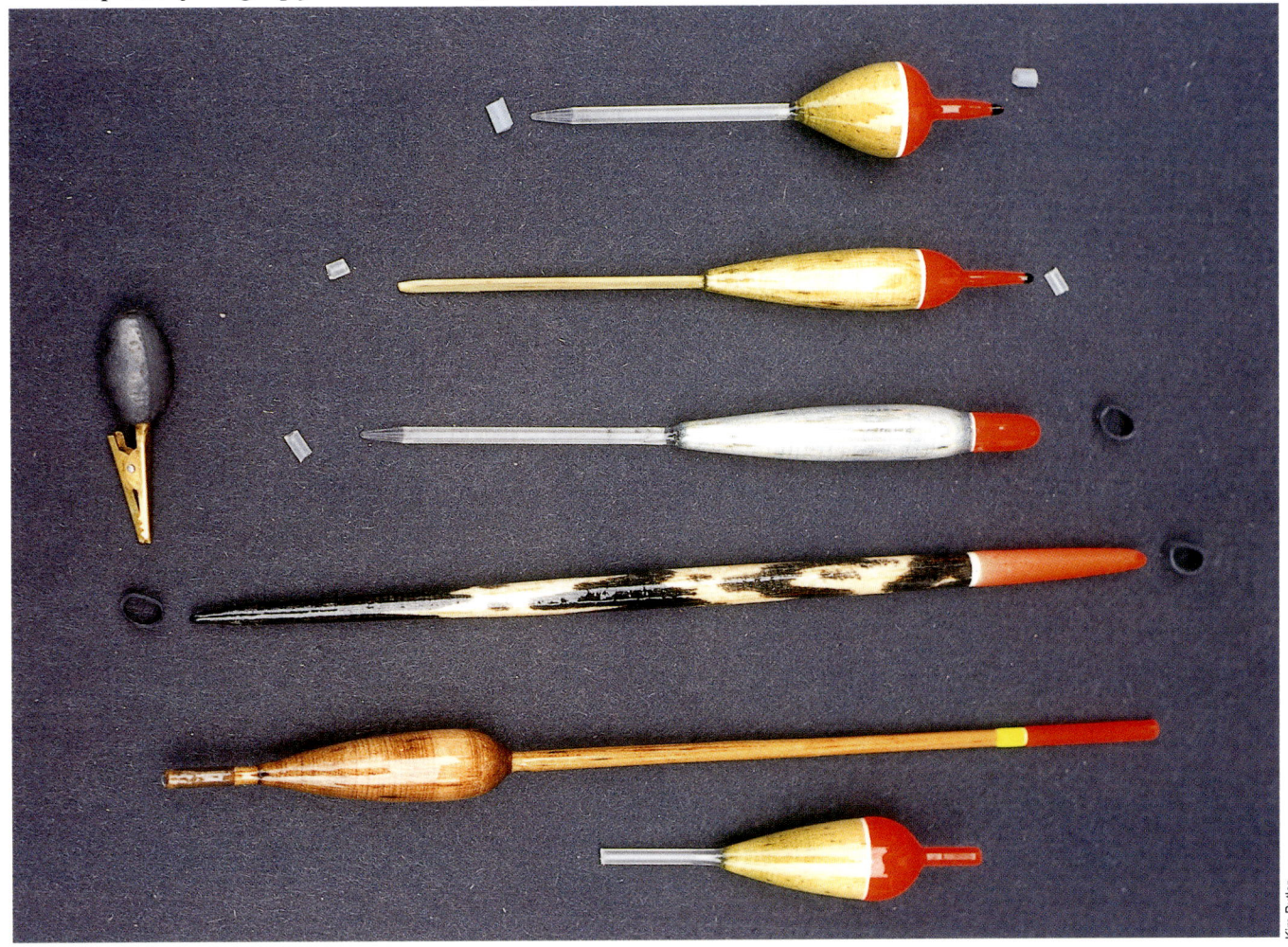

Chapter 3: Subtle Presentations | 25

water types, therefore allowing the angler to fish fast, moderate, or slow flows using the same float. It should also be noted that slow flows do not always constitute the use of long slender float styles. Most float shapes can be used throughout moderate to slow flows once given size considerations, however, keep in mind that the general rule of thumb is to use the smallest float possible to reach potential holding water. In the long run, the ultimate decision on float application will be based on the angler's confidence and previous on stream experiences.

✥ Shotting Floats Do's and Don'ts ✦

Proper shot placement below the float is usually dictated by the water in which you are fishing. Keep in mind that as a river is moving downstream the quickest flow is usually on or near the surface while the area of reduced flow is nearer the bottom. With this in mind, it only stands to reason that the larger shots are placed closer to the float and the smaller ones further down towards the hook. This setup is standard for fishing moderate to slow flows.

For faster flows, bulk up on shot further from the float but within of the hook. Quite often the standard shotting pattern is not sufficient for casting distance. In this scenario the angler may want to increase float size as added weight or simply bulk up on shot just under the float.

✥ Shot Considerations ✦

Moving from one water type to another may mean sliding shot up or down your leader line. Be careful with fluorocarbon leaders as they have a tendency to easily fray during this procedure. One way to offset this problem is not to over tighten shot once placed on the leader. Leave them a little lose or moisten the line with saliva prior to moving the shots up or down. Other considerations when loading shot underneath your float are bait and lure weight. Remember to compensate for this if you are using large roe sacs with attractors or if using bead-head flies and jigs. Generally speaking, only use enough shot to cock your float in an upright position, and perhaps, a little more but avoid going to extremes by adding so much shot that the float attains neutral buoyancy and rides the drift mostly under the stream surface. When used in this fashion, others sharing the drift won't be able to see your submerged float and the end result will undoubtedly mean frustrating tangles and downtime.

✥ Trotting ✦

Oftentimes anglers manipulate the progressive downstream movement of their floats by slightly holding back on them as they drift through areas of holding water. This technique, termed "trotting" or "checking," allows the bait, fly, or lure to proceed the terminal tackle making for a much more realistic presentation. Used in clear water, trotting may give the fish the impression of a bait that is momentarily caught in a crosscurrent or upwelling while in turbid water it allows fish ample time to spot and pursue our baits. Trotting is primarily used during fast to moderate flow situations. To trott in faster flowing water, anglers may want to increase the

Holding back on the natural downstream progression of the float allows your bait to proceed in front of the split shot and float. Also known as trotting or checking, this technique makes a more realistic presentation.

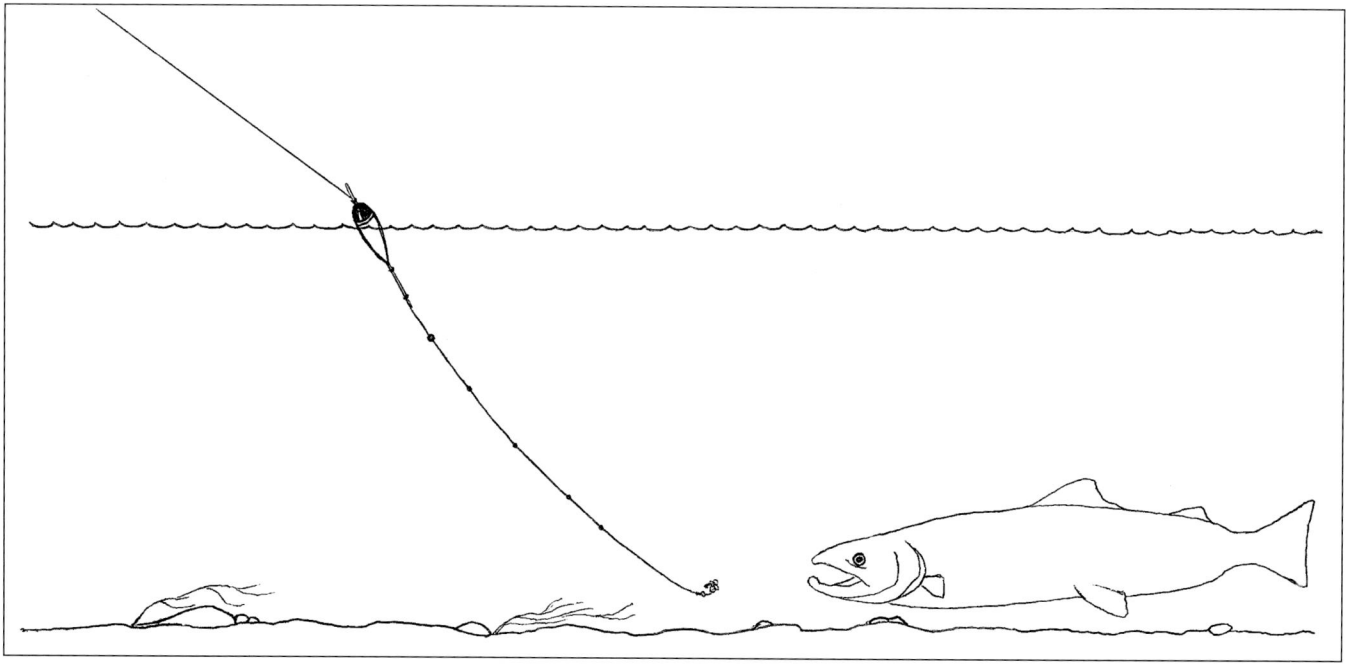

amount of line beneath the float to compensate for the greater angle of the presentation.

❧ Long Leads and Moderate Depths ☙

One of the greatest aspects of float fishing is the array of presentations that they afford us. Not only are long leads beneath our floats used for fast water trotting, but they can also be used in areas of moderate flow and depth. In this scenario, baits are literally bounced along the bottom. My first introduction to this technique was a humbling experience. An old timer and I were trying to squeeze out the last remaining days of the spring steelie season along Ontario's infamous Ganaraska River. Sharing the drift, the old timer was pulling out fish hand-over-fist and when I observed his technique I noticed that the lead beneath his float was far greater than mine when the moderate river depth was considered.

The old timer and I chatted for awhile and he informed me that this technique served him well throughout his years as a steelheader. I have often used this technique since then in various situations and am always brought back to the humble day spent with the old timer.

❧ Float Fishing and Wind Direction ☙

Float fishing for steelhead during windy conditions no doubt presents some unique and unprecedented challenges. It seems as though casting, line mending, and float control all become compromised. Hence, most anglers view the wind with a negative connotation. However, not all anglers fall into this category because some anglers view the wind as an adversary rather than a nuisance. (They often reach the point where they are constantly watching the local weather reports and checking overhead gas station flags in eager anticipation of some hot steelhead action.)

Generally speaking, windy conditions have to be given some special equipment considerations. Depending on the intensity of the wind and where you are fishing, you may want to leave the float reel at home in favor of spinning equipment. Even experienced float handlers will have difficulty casting in the wind. Float choices also play a large role in coping with persistent windy conditions. Let's take a closer look at wind directions and float choices.

❧ Upstream Winds ☙

Winds blowing across your favorite steelie stream will usually do so either from an upstream or downstream direction. Generally, upstream winds are traveling in the opposite direction of the current which often creates small riffles on the surface. Therefore, upstream winds are favored especially when using nymphs, wet fly patterns, or jigs. (The bouncing action imparted on the float due to the wave action is beneficial because it provides movement within the bait which is suggestive of a living organism.)

The most beneficial float shape to use during an upstream wind presentation would be a medium to large sized grayling. This float shape can easily catch and ride the bouncing drift as it lifts and then drops your jig or fly adding a real life-like appeal to the entire presentation.

Fishing during periods of upstream winds also requires you to re-think some angling strategies, for instance, line control. Unlike calm weather conditions, when you are able to keep your line high off the stream surface, windy conditions call for just the opposite.

Keeping your line high off the water surface during an upstream wind will succeed in pushing your presentation back upstream or it will stall in the drift. To offset this problem simply lower the rod tip and keep your line low on the stream. For the most part, you won't be in the strike zone long during an upstream wind because of the slack line you are constantly having to reel in.

The belly which you have tried to avoid—by keeping a low line profile—has now occurred on the stream surface but this is much more preferable because it is easier to rectify. To get rid of the belly, lift the line off the stream surface and lower it again so that it is parallel with the float. This technique is called line mending and is an important line control measure. (Keep working all areas of the holding water at the same time because if steelies are present you may be in for a real treat.)

Quite often a beneficial wind will only appear in short sections of a stream stretch depending on its geography. To give you an example of how deadly fishing in the wind can be I actually have steelheading friends who literally run to these sections when the wind picks up. The ironic thing is that once the intermittent winds die out they will either fish close by, but more often then not, they will break for a quick coffee or catch up on some tackle talk with other steelheaders only to run back to the same locations once the wind picks up again. It's quite comical to watch but these guys have done their homework and they are definitely in tune with steelhead behavior.

❧ Downstream Winds ☙

Downstream winds are the worst winds of all for the float fisherman, thus trying to maintain any type of control with a conventional float will only lead to frustration. In this situation the wind is traveling in the same direction as the current and in so doing will actually push a float—such as a grayling—way ahead of your terminal tackle making for a completely unnatural presentation. To conquer the downstream winds, U.K. anglers have developed float styles that actually ride subsurface with only about a half inch of stem peeking out above the stream surface. These balsa wagglers—as they are often called—resemble longer inverted versions of the avon float styles. Wagglers are not fixed on your line like a conventional float but are rather fed through a plastic hole or small loop on the bottom of the float so that your line will actually sit under the water and out of the wind. Wagglers are free-sliding floats much in the same manner of a slip float so you will require a bobber stop to keep baits in the strike zone. Balsa wagglers can also be used in upstream winds but you will not get that bouncing action that seems to excite steelhead. Again, you may want to consider leaving the float reel at home during overly windy situations in favor of spinning gear.

➔ The Strike ←

If a survey was taken among the Great Lakes float fishing fraternity on what is the most intriguing element of steelheading I bet most of the answers would all come back the same, that being watching and eagerly awaiting the float to register a strike.

No other facet of steelheading will leave you feeling as adrenalinized or as pumped as a steelhead that shows interest in your presentation. What makes it even more thrilling is the fact that a steelhead may choose to take a bait in several different fashions oftentimes leaving the steelheader scratching his head wondering just when to set the hook. Generally, steelhead strike in five different fashions.

1. The total take down: Aggressive fish often register a hit by totally submerging the float.

2. Tap and hesitation: The tap, followed by slight hesitation, then take down. This type of hit gives the angler fair warning as the slight tap is indicative of a sure take down to follow.

3. The slight tap: This hit is often so subtle that anglers not focusing on their float will never realize that they even had one.

To connect with these wary steelies I recommend setting the hook as fast as possible without waiting since a second takedown or tap is unlikely. On a further note, if you do observe a slight but fast takedown or tap, followed by the quick resurfacing of your float, set the hook anyway as often the subtle taking steelhead will still have the bait in its mouth. The key to connecting with these fish is to pay attention and to be quick on the hook set.

4. Multiple Taps and Hesitation: This one really gets the adrenaline pumping because you never know quite when to set the hook. The float will be taken under and pop up just as fast, hesitate, and then it'll be taken under only to pop up equally as fast again. This is repeated several times within the first or subsequent drifts. My best advice is to try and anticipate the next takedown and set the hook fast.

5. Weird Take Downs: The last type of take down is surely the weirdest take down of all. Quite often steelhead seem to aggressively take down our floats and upon setting the hook the angler fails to connect with the fish and is often left with a crushed roe sac. The angler repeats the drift several times with the same results, but no fish. Observing this phenomenon over the years has led me to believe that these "toying" steelhead are caught between wanting to hit but may be indecisive due to angling pressure. Just how steelies hit a drifted bait without getting hooked is beyond me especially when your roe sacs come back continually crushed. Having experimented with these indecisive Steelies over the years I have found them to be extremely cooperative once you offer them a horizontal presentation in the form of lures instead of offering them a drifted vertical presentation that they may have already been stung on earlier.

➔ Long Drifts and Hook Sets ←

On occasion when you are fortunate enough to have a stream section to yourself you may want to take some extended drifts. However doing so undoubtedly means that slack line will occur throughout your drift.

Fresh, aggressive fish will hammer a presentation and totally sink a float. As their stream stay becomes longer and fishing pressure increases, fish may take a more subtle approach to feeding habits. Never take your eyes off a drifting float. Chris Atkinson displays a Nottawasaga autumn chromer.

Nothing in float fishing leaves you feeling more helpless than having your float go down and not being able to set the hook because of the slack line between you and your float. The best one can do is to mend their line, however, setting the hook during extended drifts requires you to deviate from the norm. Setting the hook straight back works great when your float is slightly up or downstream from your standing position but during the extended drift doing so will only succeed in pulling the bait straight out of the steelhead's mouth. Instead, set the hook low and sideways, left or right depending on your positioning on the bank or in the water. Setting the hook in this manner often connects with the corner of the steelhead's mouth and reduces the chances of not connecting. This technique helped me to land one of my largest steelhead ever. Drifting my float downstream yielded a complete take down but because of conditioning I set the hook straight back and never even connected with the fish. The fish took the bait once again on the next drift but this time I side set and connected with a brute male steelhead all of 24 pounds (10.9kg).

➔ Plumbing Out Pools ←

Perhaps one of the most important fish catching tools that I own in my steelheading arsenal is the simple plumb bomb. I can't stress enough the importance of these inexpensive, highly productive tools but most steelheaders I know aren't even aware of what they are or what they do. Simply put, a plumb bomb is a heavy weight that attaches to your hook which will sink your float once in the stream. Their intended use is to give the angler a perception of a pool's depth.

To determine depth throw the float and plumb bomb into a pool. If the whole rig sinks then the float needs to be adjusted or moved up your line until it sits just under the stream's surface. A float sitting on top of the surface means you have over gauged the depth. This accurate reading of a pool's depth will keep your baits in the strike zone once steelies head for the stream bottoms with the onset of cold weather. I can't tell you how many times anglers fish slow, deep pools without knowing their true depths. These same anglers are also going fishless when they otherwise could be having an awesome day.

Don't bother buying a plumb bomb because they are the simplest thing to make. All that is needed is a 1/4 or 1/2 ounce (7-14g) egg sinker and some alligator clips which can be purchased at most electrical stores. Peel the red or black plastic handles off with a pair of pliers, exposing the metal handle, then simply insert it into the end of an egg sinker. It should be a snug fit. You can easily make a dozen plumb bombs for around five bucks. Always carry a few with you in case you lose one on the river bottom. Also, always plumb out the bottom of your favorite holes on subsequent outings because of fluctuating water conditions. I absolutely never leave home without a few of these underutilized, inexpensive productive tools. In a nutshell, they will be your ace in the hole during the cold weather period.

➔ Slip Floats ←

Once steelhead re-locate to the bottom of pools to ride out the winter then switching to slip floats may be the only logical way to reach them. A standard float setup may not be feasible since a pools depth may equal or exceed that of your rod and subsequent lead. Using a slip float, by which the line can easily slide through, and a pre-fixed neoprene bobber stop that can be adjusted up or down the line according to the pools depth, you can easily overcome your deep drifting dilemma.

Since the prefixed neoprene bobber stop easily slides through guides and onto the spool, the angler is afforded a far easier cast since he now only has a few feet of leader line under his float instead of 10 or more feet. Once the float enters the drift, the split shot and bait will pull line through the hollow slip float tube until being halted by the bobber stop. Be sure to affix the bobber stop far enough up the line to equal the pool's depth. Use a plumb bomb to determine depth.

Chris Weland and the result of fishing within the strike zone.

➤ Today's Floats ⭠

Today's floats don't allow you to catch any more fish than in the past. Most tackle shops around the Great Lakes seem to carry a wide assortment of float shapes and styles from around globe. Some tackle shops may even carry a homemade selection of floats from crafty regional steelheaders. As of late, the steelheading trend seems to be geared towards the use of all clear plastic float models which are a great concept for fishing during today's low and clear water conditions, however, having done extensive experimenting with regular balsa brands, I have concluded that there really is no clear advantage in the use of these all clear plastic float brands. Steelhead are rarely concerned with what might be floating on top of the stream surface, especially during turbid conditions or while sitting in deep over-wintering pools. Even post-spawn steelhead suspended only a foot or two below calm slow-moving water don't seem to be bothered with what's on the surface so long as they are not over pressured in which case even the shadow from an overhead bird will send them scattering throughout the pool. Anglers need to be more concerned with what is presented beneath their floats since this is where the steelhead's attention will be focused.

If I had to choose between balsa floats or the clear plastic variety, balsa would win every time. They are light, inexpensive, colorful works of art which have served me well throughout all steelhead seasons. The plastic variety are expensive, may leak, and some anglers even suggest that sunlight radiating through the float can spook steelhead. Regardless of float models or materials the ultimate choice will lie within the steelheader's preference and his confidence level. For those, such as myself, who prefer the balsa variety, I have included a chapter on how to make your own floats at home. They are simple to make, inexpensive, and anyone can easily make enough in one day to last the entire season.

➤ Additional Float Considerations ⭠

- Never take your eyes off a drifting float, you will miss more fish this way than any other.
- Keep line high off the water and maintain float control whenever possible.
- Use three pieces of silicone tubing on your float in case one breaks.
- Popping or snapping a float at the end of a drift is not necessary because it only spooks fish.

Chapter 4
Natural and Artificial Bait

❖ Roe ❖

Roe is unquestionably the hands down favorite bait of the Great Lakes steelheader, and for good reason. As juveniles, Great Lake steelhead get their first introduction to free drifting eggs in their first autumn of stream life when stocks of salmon have began to seed the tributaries. Free drifting eggs must be met with eager enthusiasm as yet another feeding opportunity presenting itself to these young fish. Egg eating opportunities once again appear as adult steelhead and other spring spawning fish take their turn on the spawning beds during this period. So as you can see, feeding on free drifted eggs quickly becomes a staple in the steelhead's feeding regime at a tender age. Although this is the most reasonable explanation as to why our steelhead love to snack on roe, it may not be the only reason.

Looking back to when a steelhead was in its infancy during the alevien or sac fry stage of its life, its first introduction to food was the contents of its own embryonic fluids. Perhaps they have catalogued this and show a propensity towards its taste. It seems anglers often prefer steelhead roe as their long-term bait of choice but during certain times of the year roe from other salmonid species, such as autumn running salmon, brown and lake trout, are also favored. Carrying a couple of different roe varieties—i.e. coho or brown roe—oftentimes means an extra fish or two.

Roe use across the Great Lakes often differs from that of our West Coast counterparts but the end results are the same. Steelhead across the Great Lakes depend more on fresh roe tied into soft sacs which is better suited to our slower, often shallower clearer flows as opposed to West Coast anglers who are fishing larger, deeper, faster flows.

Skeined chunks cured using a variety of different ingredients, scents and oils are often preferred by our West Coast contemporaries. Cures are used as a measure to preserve and toughen up the skeins which are cut into sizable chunks and secured to the hook using an egg loop. These skein chunks are then fished under a float, bottom bounced with corkies and yarn, or fished off the bottom with attractors such as winged Spin n Glos.

Fresh roe presentations are often top bait choices for Great Lakes steelheaders

Scrapping mature skeins (egg slide down) with a tablespoon is often the most productive method of removing eggs from the skein membrane

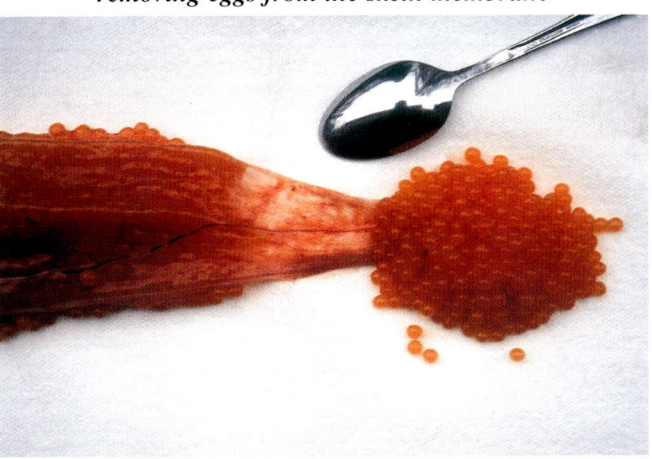

Chapter 4: Natural and Artificial Bait | 31

Fishing skein chunks for Great Lakes steelhead is not a common practice since smaller baits and hooks are often the norm and as such, securing a small skein chunk via the egg loop to a small hook can become a tedious task especially during the colder months. For those eager to try preserved skein egg clusters on Great Lakes steelhead, try using them during high turbid water situations with larger hooks as they are easier to work with on this level.

For the most part, Great Lakes steelheaders prefer to scrape the ripening eggs out of the mature skein membrane then tie the loose eggs in colorful commercial roe netting material. In this manner, egg sacs can be tied to match varying water conditions using a variety of colors. On the downside, in order to obtain quality mature skeins one must dispatch the fish which is a poor conservation practice especially on rivers containing self sustaining wild populations of steelhead. A good alternative is to catch and retain a hatchery fish which is less of a loss to the river than a wild fish that was bred with locally adapted traits which are conducive to that specific river environment. Another good alternative is to use roe from salmon which are also a stocked fish. However, if your choice is steelie eggs then the following will help explain which fish contain mature skeins. In order to differentiate between quality mature skeins of ripening fish versus the small pin head skein of immature fish there are some physical features to look for. First of all, look at the body color and condition of the fish. The darker the hen, the more likely it is to contain ripening eggs. Also, observe the anal vent, maturing eggs will often push the vent out from the body. Lastly, also look for plumpness within the belly area. Close to egg maturation the belly may look strangely full close to the fish's vent, while further up the belly, the fullness has disappeared. This is a sure sign that the skein has ripened and eggs have begun to separate, some may have also spilled from the vent and onto the bank when you handled your fish.

Once you have decided to keep a hen for eggs and consumption, then care must be given to the eggs immediately. First and foremost you need to bleed the fish to remove all blood from the eggs. This can be done simply by nicking or cutting out the gills. Removing blood from the eggs will help to keep the eggs from spoiling and give them a longer fridge life especially if you are going to use them within two to three weeks. Depending on the circumstances, some may wish to remove the eggs soon after the fish has been bled especially in warmer temps, however if cooler temps prevail, all should be fine until you arrive home.

Most Great Lakes steelheaders, myself included, do not preserve eggs as our West Coast cohorts do. This is mainly due to our more gentle flowing tributaries where fish have ample time to scrutinize, accept, or reject our egg offerings. Often, steelhead will spit out eggs that feel hard when mouthed, so we go with the real deal opting not to use preservatives which harden roe. Below is my no fail method for storing scraped mature steelhead skiened eggs for future outings.

First of all I absolutely never rinse my skeins off with water. If you have bled the fish properly then there is no need to, besides, why would you want to wash all the great scent down the drain. Next I lay down some layers of newspapers, then place a couple of absorbent white shop towels (which are similar to your everyday home brand of paper towel but more absorbent), over the top of the newspaper. (A roll of towels can be purchased at some of the larger hardware chains, for a couple of dollars.) You may or may not want to use latex gloves at this point to help eliminate human scent from the eggs though this is personal preference.

Next, lay the mature skein eggs side down, gently scraping the eggs out the end of the skein membrane with a small tablespoon. Scrapping eggs may take some time, so do not rush since you will only succeed in scrapping out clumps of skeined eggs rather than individual eggs.

Once all the eggs are scrapped out, roll them around on some fresh shop towels to help whisk away moisture. On another table, lay down some fresh newsprint and on top lay down more fresh absorbent shop towels. Take the scrapped eggs and transfer just enough eggs onto the fresh towel so they can be spread out. By spreading the eggs out by hand you will help them air dry quicker which is the goal we are trying to achieve. You will want to roll the eggs around by hand throughout the drying process so that all eggs dry equally on all sides. Some small to mid-size egg clumps may appear in the beginning, this indicates that the eggs are wet so spread them out as best you can.

Drying time takes about three hours. However, take caution as not to over dry to the point where the eggs will shrivel up and harden. Generally, you want the eggs to feel dry and tacky. Eggs that are too moist will surely break once thawed so be sure they are just right before freezing. Once the eggs have been dried properly we can move onto the next step. The next step requires the use of real cheap aluminum foil that can be bought at most dollar stores. The key is cheap because it seems the cheap stuff is the thinnest and most flexible which is ideal for our intended use. Cut off enough aluminum foil to wrap one or two day outings worth of roe. Place the shinny side down as to help guard against frost. Next place the eggs in the foil and wrap snug but not so tight as to break any eggs. You also want to wrap the tag ends of the foil so that they are underneath the finished package. Next, place several foil wrapped egg packs into a large zip-lock freezer bag and suck all the air out with a straw. Put this into another large freezer bag and suck the air out of this also. Your eggs are now ready for the freezer. Once thawed you may want to rub some scent such as oil of anise on your hands prior to tying up your eggs and again prior to fishing but this is all personal preference.

Although this process may take quite some time to complete, it is well worth the effort since it produces quality soft natural fresh looking eggs which are ideally suited for our moderate flows and often finicky steelhead. Eggs will last up to a half hour on the hook without whitening out.

➔ Roe on the Run ←

On those occasions when you have acquired fresh skiens but can't dedicate the time for scrapping and freezing there is a short term alternative. First and foremost once again bleed the fish and remove skiens at home, then pat them dry using the absorbent shop towel, as before. Next roll each skien into a fresh piece of shop towel and fold the ends. Wrap again, this time using newspaper, and don't forget to fold the ends. Place each wrapped skien into a separate freezer bag sucking out all the air, then place in the fridge. The newspaper absorbs moisture from condensation while the shop towel absorbs moisture from the eggs. These stored eggs have a refrigerator life of about 3 weeks though after a couple of days skiens become unscrappable as they begin to break down. At this point the skeined eggs are still of value, but they have to be cut or pealed into small chunks then tied.

You have to do a lot of fishing in order to make full use of all this roe so my advice is to set aside some time to scrape and freeze as previously discussed.

➔ Salmon Roe ←

Although steelhead and brown roe are the eggs of choice for most of the year, it is hard to beat Chinook or coho salmon roe for early to mid autumn steelhead fishing. However, Chinook roe really doesn't freeze well unless it is preserved. If you like the fresh stuff, then try obtaining enough loose eggs to match the frequency of your outings, otherwise preserve the eggs in a commercial or home brew cure.

➔ Foul Smelling Eggs ←

Foul smelling eggs, the kind that form sinking vapor clouds when you remove the jar lid, can often turn out to be some of the best roe on the river. Generally, tied eggs that have been left over from previous outings usually fall into this category. Although the "fresh is best" adage is accepted as the norm do not discount these "wake the dead" smelling eggs as they often outperform the fresh stuff.

Case in point: A relative with very little fishing experience, (he preferred that the spinning reel be used upside down as opposed to the traditional method), accompanied me on a steelhead trip several years ago and instead of tying him up some fresh stuff I let him use the stinky roe that I had left over and was ready to throw out. Needless to say my awkward looking relative had a banner day often yelling for me to help him land his fish. Since then, I have often used the stinky stuff with good results.

➔ Store-Bought Egg Cures ←

Store bought egg cures and scents seem to be more popular around the Pacific Northwest as opposed to most areas of the Great Lakes. Most commercial cures seem to use dyes, sulfites, and sugar as ingredients in these cures which preserve and toughen the skeins making them more durable when casted into the heavier West Coast flows. The speedy currents often leave fish little time to scrutinize between naturally soft or toughened up cured eggs and therefore produce better results out West than they do across the tributaries of the Great Lakes. I have experimented with store bought egg cures with mixed results and found that it is hard to beat a soft natural egg presentation for Great Lakes steelhead. Egg cures do however offer a quick solution for the long term storage of eggs that can be left at the bottom of the fridge ready to tie on at a moments notice.

➔ Making Sense of Scents ←

Since we have already established that steelhead can smell on average three parts per million, the question remains how much of an effect will this have in terms of how we handle our natural or artificial baits. My immediate answer is very little, and I can back that statement up with two decades of steelhead experience. However, this is not to say that you shouldn't take care and use caution when handling your baits. I, for one, would not expose my roe to any obnoxious odors because contamination could occur. Having scrapped and tied thousands of roe bags, both with and without latex gloves to cover my scent, and both with and without added scents, I can truthfully tell you that I did no better or worse in terms of my angling success. But consider this, on rare occasions I have witnessed anglers picking up an extra fish soon after applying a little scent to their eggs. On the other hand, I have had equal success using artificials with no added scents. I have found that the use of commercial scents on our eggs and artificials is more a matter of personal choice rather than a necessity. Will I stop trying scents? No, as a matter of fact I plan on trying more magic potions simply because I love to experiment and see what will or will not work.

↣ Roe Tying Materials ↢

Tying loose eggs into small to mid-sized roe sacs is a common practice for the Great Lakes steelheader but, there are a couple of different materials to chose from and you may wonder if one is better than the other. One of the first commercial materials to hit the tackle stores was a soft supple mesh material which till this day continues to catch steelhead. However, prior to its inception some anglers were already using women's nylon hair scarves that were found in local department stores. Today these scarves have also made their way into many a Great Lakes tackle shop. The only difference between the two materials is that the nylon scarf has a tighter weave as opposed to the mesh which gives the eggs a little more detail, but my experience has taught me that steelies are most interested in the overall appearance and natural scent of the eggs over the extreme detail.

In areas that sustain heavy angling pressure using the tightly woven scarf material may yield an additional fish but, by that time, fish are likely tempted to take other offerings. Something to consider when deciding upon which cloth to use is that the nylon scarves often take twice as long to wrap because you have to use several half hitches of thread to knot the top of the finished sac. The other material can simply be wrapped with several turns of elastic thread then easily snapped off. Unfortunately, the elastic thread does not hold well on the scarves, often letting loose while casting, leaving you with an empty roe sac. I tend to favor the latter when wrapping my eggs as they make for a quick and easy tie which produces favorable results. In the end, the decision will be yours. Go with what you have the most confidence in. Invariably there are gadgets on the market that will assist in the roe tying process and if the truth be told they are not needed as roe can be easily tied by hand. Simply add the desired amount of eggs into the center of a two-inch-square piece (5cm) of roe mesh then grab all four corners and give the cloth a slight twist to help ball the eggs up. Apply several wraps of elastic thread around the top of the roe sac and snap off. Remember, use elastic thread with the store bought roe mesh as it will not hold up well on the scarf material. For scarf material use either household sewing thread or commercial silk thread found in most tackle store. Both can be wrapped in a similar fashion to the elastic thread with the addition of a series of half hitches to secure the knot.

↣ Roe Colors ↢

Netting material used for tying roe sacs comes in a variety of colors ranging from florescent shades to more natural, subdued hues. While steelhead will accept most of these colored egg presentations, they often times seem to show rather distinct preferences for specific colors during certain times of the year.

Having pursued Great Lakes steelhead for two decades I have learned that fresh run steelhead display a natural affinity for the colors pink and

Roe tying material varies from women's scarves to store bought commercial netting.

Roe wrapped in various mesh colors often produces favorable results. Paul Shimano holds a "high teens" late autumn male that took a red roe sac.

chartreuse (bright green) however, often in variable shades. I have also learned that rarely do these two colors work during the same periods throughout the seasons as it is often either or. We will discuss this more in the seasonal section.

One major misconception that a lot of anglers make while fishing for fresh run steelhead is that the more natural tones of peach, white, yellow etc. should be used in clear water as they appear less alarming and more naturally suited to the water conditions. While this sounds like a sensible choice, it appears that fresh run steelhead have their own agendas and often do not see things from our perspective. More often than not it is the stale fish that seems to be more accepting of the smaller more naturally colored tones.

On the other hand, friends and I have experimented in clear water with some oddball colors that have also proven worthy of note. Red was a wise choice for one of my buddies who took an autumn run steelhead in the high teens from a heavily fished pool. On other occasions we have used blue with some success and as of late light purple (scarf material) has also been producing favorable results. All experimenting aside, stick to the known producers pink and chartreuse. For fresh run fish we will take a closer look at using roe during turbid conditions in the seasonal sections.

✥ Final Thoughts on Roe Use ✥

The use of roe as bait throughout the Great Lakes region is often the topic of much controversy and debate. While most are in favor of its use there are those voicing to ban it citing that the overuse of eggs by an increasing number of anglers may be harming the fishery, thus lending to its demise.

While the over exploitation of our fishery may be valid, there appears to be other governing factors such as habitat loss, climate change, and shifting forage bases that seem to be conspiring against our Great Lakes steelhead and as such I urge everyone to make responsible decisions regarding the number of fish that are kept for egg use and consumption.

Although roe will always reign supreme with many Great Lakes steelheaders, the use of artificials can, and often do, outperform the best egg presentations.

Following, in the bait section, I will explain how the use of artificials under a float are often responsible for nearly 100% of my daily catches, and although I am in no way condemning the use of roe, there are times I wonder why I even brought it.

✥ Worms ✥
The Other Natural Bait

Following close behind roe, the lowly worm gets the nod as being the second most widely accepted natural bait. However, not all worms sold in tackle shops today can be classified as worms in the true sense as essentially they are the larvae of developing insects that have fallen into the category of worms. Nevertheless, they have all become time-tested baits and have earned their rightful place in this book.

Below is a description of the more popular worm types and when to fish them.

✥ Earthworms ✥

Otherwise known as dew worms or nightcrawlers, earthworms are probably the most widely recognized worm simply because of their abundant distribution and their effectiveness for tempting steelhead. Their rather robust size offers added eye appeal and can be used in part or whole depending on both water conditions and angling pressure. What has always intrigued me about the use of these large worms is their effectiveness on steelhead during low, clear water periods when rain has been absent for weeks. It may appear unnatural that a worm would get washed into the flow during such a time but it is quite evident that undisturbed steelhead seem to care much less about how the worm got there and seem to be more interested in securing the easy meal. This revealing behavior is a true testament to a steelhead's opportunistic behavior. Do not neglect to use dew worms for post-spawners either, especially after a good spring rain which colors the water. This is often the best time to use them. Store dewies in a cool place (fridge or basement) as they do not fair well in warmer temps.

✥ Red Wigglers ✥

Red wigglers, also known as trout or manure worms, are on the opposite side of the spectrum when compared to the dew worm. Wigglers only grow to between 1 1/2 to 2 1/2 inches (3.8-6.4cm) in length and are rather thin in nature, but what they lack in comparable size they more than make up for in vigor. Once placed on the hook they literally try and squirm off (hence the name wigglers) which makes them especially appealing to post-spawn spring steelies suspended in clear, slow-moving pools. Fish them on tiny #16 hooks and set the hook immediately upon any indication of a takedown. Remember these are small worms so steelies will inhale them quickly. Short of purchasing the lethal wiggler from your local tackle shop, you may find them in piles of manure feeding upon small undigested bits of grain and grass. At the end of the steelhead season wigglers can be easily kept in your backyard compost. As an added bonus, heat from your compost will keep your wigglers healthy and mating all winter long providing you with enough bait for years to come.

➔ Wax Worms ←

Wax worms are not true worms at all, in fact they are not even related. Being members of the insect family wax worms are in the larval stage prior to becoming a moth. Their 3/4 inch (1.9cm) size, soft bodies and milky white to tan appearance, closely mimic that of the native stream-dwelling caddis larvae which is prominent throughout most Great Lakes tributaries. Wax worms also closely mimic blow fly larvae better known as the common house fly which lay their eggs on top of partially submerged carcasses of dead salmon or steelhead. Once the eggs hatch into larvae they frequently lose their footing and are washed down to eagerly awaiting steelhead. Given that wax worms closely mimic some natural food sources it's easy to see why they have become part of a steelheader's arsenal.

Generally speaking, wax worms are the favored springtime bait often used for stubborn post -pawn steelhead that have seen too much of everything else. For optimal results thread several of these bite-sized baits onto a #14 hook and fish them throughout slow-flowing pools. For suspended fish, try using the trotting technique discussed in Chapter Three. For best results, store wax worms at room temperature as they seem to become lethargic when cooled.

➔ Meal Worms ←

Like wax worms the meal worm is a member of the insect family that is in the larval stage prior to becoming a beetle. They range anywhere from one to two inches and are tanish in color. Although I have used meal worms in the past, I did not favor them because of their hard shell-like body surface and because I found other baits more suitable.

➔ The Artificial Advantage ←

Although roe has become the bait of choice for the majority of Great Lakes steelheaders, it is far from the only bait that will produce fish on a consistent basis. As a matter of fact, steelhead may actually turn off of roe during certain periods throughout the year due to angling pressure or in order to search for other seasonal feeding opportunities.

Once steelhead decide to switch feeding modes it is often the "tuned in" angler, suspending artificials beneath their floats, that generally prevails. These anglers have learned to think outside of the box and as a result have taken their steelhead skills to a whole new level. These same anglers have a

Wax Worms: Resembling a number of smaller streamside invertibrates, wax worms make great clear water baits. For best results thread 3 worms onto a small #14 or 16 hook.
Meal Worms: Available at pet supply stores, meal worms also produce their share of steelhead. Meal worms can grow to large sizes so use appropriate hook size.
Red Wigglers: Smallish in size, red wigglers squirm relentlessly once on the hook, Fish them on small #14 to 16 hooks.
Dew Worms: Use in part or whole depending on water clarity and angling pressure. Hook sizes vary according to worm length but #10 to 12 hooks should suffice.

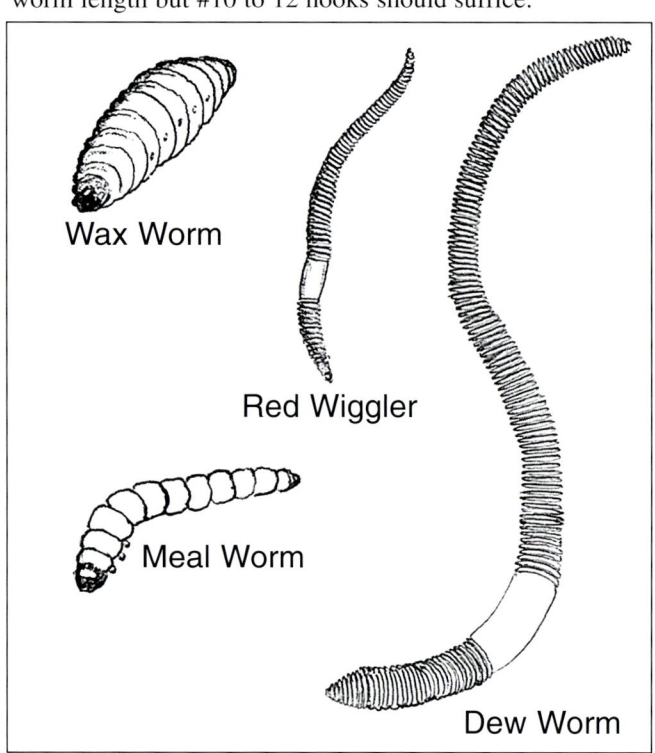

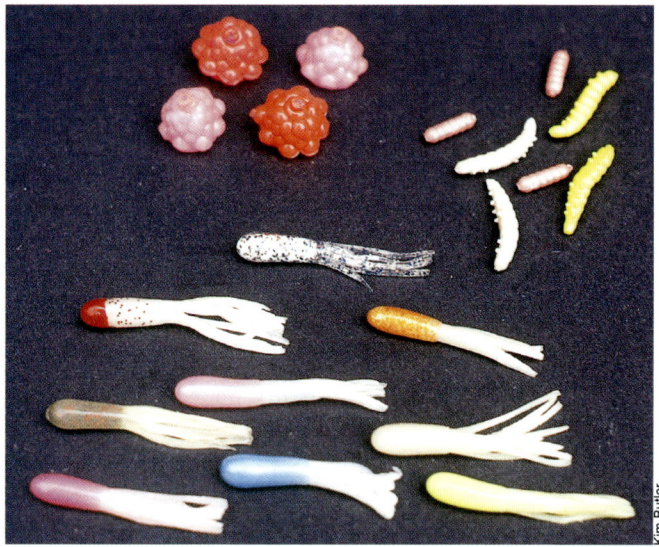

Steelhead can be taken on a variety of plastic counterfeit presentations. Pearl pink and orange Gooey Bob (upper left) often take Great Lakes steelhead in a variety of flow and turbidity levels. In clear water situations, realistic grub imitations (right) make great subtle presentations while tube jigs (bottom) fool fish in both clear and stained water.

broader perspective of a steelhead's varying dietary preferences and seasonal behaviors which has often put them way ahead of the crowd. However, the use of artificials has been slow to catch on around the Great Lakes simply because most steelheaders seem to be trapped by their past successes and can't seem to bring themselves to try non-traditional tactics given that most of their previous triumphs have come from roe.

Those that remain vigilant with roe use, even when it fails to produce, are often limiting their own success. Quite often these anglers can literally leave the river with almost as many roe sacs as they came with, while those remaining versatile with their artificial counterfeits may be cashing in on some of the best steelheading around. So why aren't more Great Lakes steelheaders making the switch to artificials? The simple answer is confidence. I can't begin to explain the number of times I have hooked steelhead alongside locals who ask me what I am using. After explaining that the fish hit an artificial they are quick to relate that they have no confidence in their use, or that they only use roe.

For those of you sitting on the fence contemplating whether or not to use artificials but you are still reluctant to do so, perhaps the following will give you a little more incentive. Despite the record low water levels and unusual temperatures that plagued Ontario during the 2002 steelhead season my most prolific presentations turned out to be artificials suspended beneath a float.

Looking over my 2002 records it turns out that artificials alone yielded me in excess of 200 steelhead. Normally, I wouldn't divulge such numbers, however, if it helps to give you some added incentive, or a little more confidence in the use of artificials, then it is well worth mentioning.

Below is a list and description of artificials that are known top steelhead producers.

➔ Gooey Bobs ⇐

Although not as popular throughout the Great Lakes as it is in the Pacific Northwest, gooey bobs have earned a well-respected place in my pocket of tricks especially when fishing during turbid water conditions. Gooey bobs are small plastic egg clusters with a piece of hollow plastic running through the middle for easy line placement. Gooey's make great attractors when steelhead waters are running high and dirty. They also work great on their own.

➔ Plastic Grubs ⇐

As of late, some intuitive tackle manufacturers have clued into the many natural food items contained within a steelhead's in-stream diet. The size, shape, color, and texture of these plastic grub-like imitations are highly suggestive of caddis and hellgrammite larvae found throughout rivers. Plastic grubs are also suggestive of blow fly larvae found on top of rotting streamside fish carcasses. Many no doubt lose their footing and end up washing into the river. Plastic grubs, of course, can also imitate a variety of tree dwelling caterpillars that are wind swept into the river as well. Try plastic grub imitations as they are quickly becoming a hot natural bait alternative.

➔ Tube Jigs ⇐

Better known as crappie baits, it didn't take long for some Ontario anglers to discover that tube jigs suspended beneath their sensitive floats were equally effective in producing limit catches of migratory steelhead. For those who've not yet tried tube jigs they are a colorful hollow plastic bait with a skirted tail. Tube jigs generally range from 1-2 inches (2.5-5cm) with the 1 1/2 inch (3.8cm) model being the standard size. Go smaller for clear water and vise versa for stained water.

For the most part tube jigs are suggestive of baitfish, shrimp, or aquatic nymphs thus making them lethal on steelhead. Some top regional colors are pearl white, pearl white/red, pearl pink, chartreuse, black, smoke/sparkle, glow in the dark, and a whole host of other color combinations.

➔ Jig Flies ⇐

The jig fly is reminiscent of the standard woolly bugger fly pattern, the exception being that it is tied on a jig hook with the addition of a brass beadhead. The jig fly differs somewhat from the standard marabou jig because of varying materials used as part of the tying pattern. Jig flies often emulate a myriad of instream invertebrates, some of which include the nymphs of dragonflies, mayflies, and stoneflies.

➔ Marabou Jigs ⇐

Perhaps one of the most seductive clear water artificials is the marabou jig. Simply blowing on one of these jigs makes it appear as though it is a living organism. Therefore, you can only imagine what it must look like to an opportunistic steelhead underwater. The pulsating movements of the marabou

Rigging the tube.

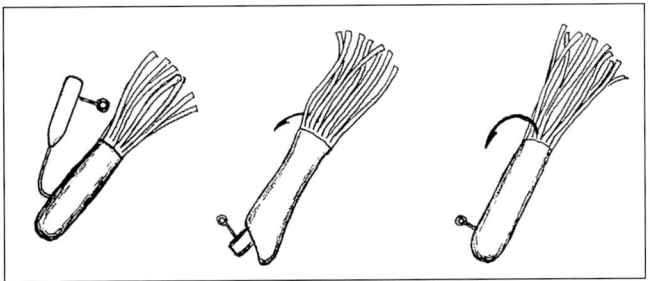

Both jig flies and marabou jig presentations are highly suggestive of naturally occuring invertibrates. Steelhead find their pulsating qualities all too real and often can't resist the temptation.

often trigger feeding behaviors in fish. Steelhead may hit these pulsating baits out of instinct, sheer aggression, or competition, all of which may relate back to its juvenile behavior when anything that looked like food, or even moved, was quickly preyed upon. Like the jig fly, marabou jigs are absolutely lethal weapons when placed under the floats of experienced steelheaders.

✦ Twisters and Marabou ✦

Prior to tying and experimenting with my own marabou jigs I began to experiment with doctored twister tails and marabou back in 1992 with favorable results. These jigs can easily be made at home. Purchase some two-inch black twister tails, some lead-head jigs, along with marabou and spider thread, (same thread used for tying roe). Assemble twister onto hook and leave a small space in front of the head. Next, cut some marabou tufts and wrap them with the spider thread just behind the jig head.

✦ Pink Plastic Worms ✦

Marty Fisher was perhaps the first steelheader in Ontario to implement the use of pink worms as part of his steelhead arsenal. Having told me about them many years ago along Ontario's Ganaraska River, I have been successfully using them ever since. Unavailable throughout Ontario tackle shops at that time, I had to order my first pink worms in British Columbia. It wouldn't be until the following spring that I was able to get a first hand account of what Marty Fisher meant about these unusual plastic presentations. Having rigged up a four inch (10.2cm) British Columbia pink paddle tail worm, I was a little hesitant to use it at first. My hesitation escalated to slight embarrassment when the landowner, and one-time steelhead guru, decided to wash some freshly picked fiddleheads nearby. Despite the landowners strange stares, all my inhibitions about using this new bait soon disappeared as I quickly connected with two post-spawn steelhead back to back.

Why pink worms are so productive I can only hazard to guess. Perhaps when left in the drift long enough real worms fade from their natural brown coloration, then take on lighter pink hues.

Today, pink worms are just now starting to show up with more frequency throughout Great Lakes tackle shops.

One of my favorite pink worms being produced today is made by Storm Tackle. Storm has taken pink-worm fishing to the next level by adding aniseed scent to the worm along with a small rattle. Although these three inch (7.6cm) baby pink worms work great on their own, the addition of scent and sound is sure to coax otherwise wary fish into hitting.

Steelheaders should be interested to know that although shades of pink are productive plastic worm colors, other colors such as white chartreuse and brown, can be equally productive. My advice is not to limit yourself to only one color and experiment when you get the chance.

✦ Rigging Plastic Worms ✦

There are a number of ways to rig plastic worms. My favorite method involves rigging the worm so that it hangs upside down. The reason I prefer this method is because the tail will hang and bob around during the drift producing instinctive strikes. This rigging method has produced more steelhead for me over the years than any other.

To begin rigging, thread your line through a large two inch (5cm) sewing needle and tie it off. Next, hold the worm upside down so that the tail hangs down and insert the needle approximately one-third the way in from the hanging tail. Work the needle through the body then exit approximately one-third of the way down. Cut the line from the needle and add either a round plastic bead or a tiny neoprene bobber stop to the line prior to tying on the hook. This will help prevent the hook

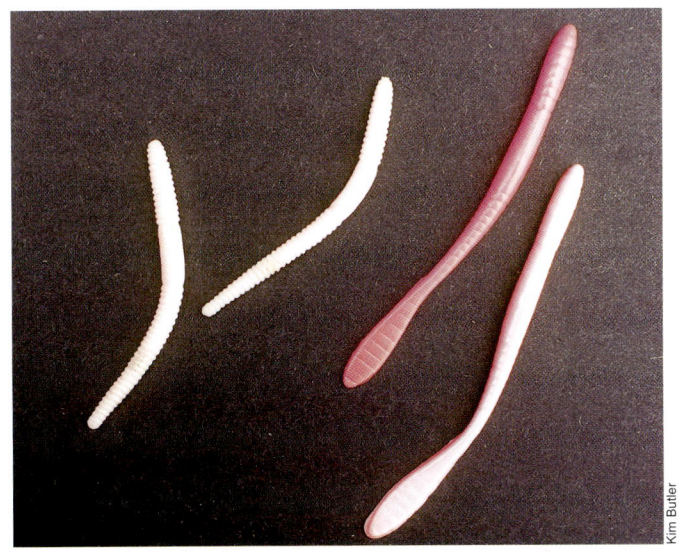

Pink plastic worms are becoming popular artificial alternatives throughout many regions, Storm's new pink worms (left) and British Columbia paddle tail worms (right) are Great Lakes favorites.

from ridding back into the worm. Contrary to how most rig their worms, I like to leave the last one-third of line dangling parallel to the tip of the worm's hanging head. This is my personal preference simply because I find that I can connect with more fish when the hook is a little more exposed then if it were snug flush directly under the worm.

Rigging Plastic Worms: Hold worm so that tail is hanging upside down. Insert needle into worm approximately 1/3 of the way and exit at 1/3 before worm head. Add a bead or a neoprene bobber stop to avoid hook from riding back into the worm. Allow line and hook to hang just below worm head for best results.

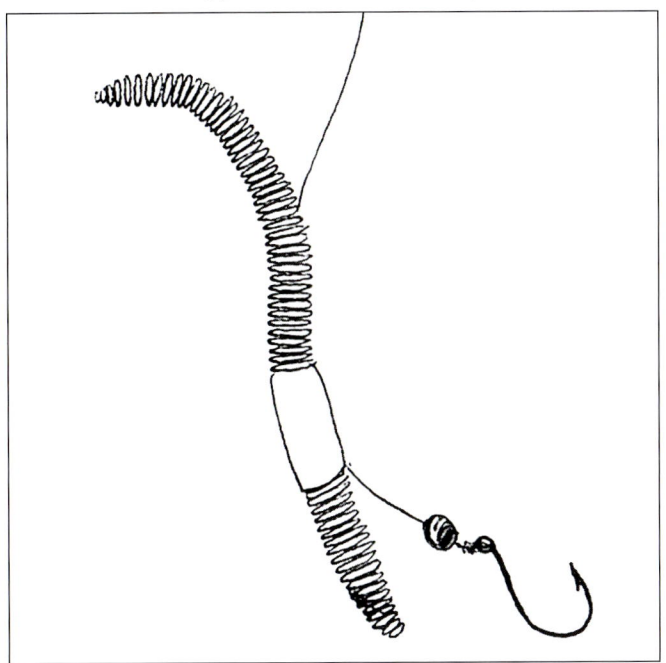

For Great Lakes regional applications two to four inch (5-10cm) plastic worms seem to work the best. As for hooks, do not be afraid to go with large 10 or 8 sizes. Plastic worms work great in both clear and turbid water situations. But one thing to keep in mind is that being made from plastic, they are rather buoyant, therefore, special consideration as to where and how we fish them needs to be addressed. For faster flowing river sections with broken water you can try bulking up on shot to within a foot of the worm. You can also try standing at the top or head of faster water, using the trotting technique as discussed in the float section.

✧ Kwikfish ✧

Often referred to as banana baits because of their shape, these wobbling plugs can make or break your day depending on water temperatures. Steelhead hammer these baits on a slow retrieve. Also, try holding or trotting them under a float. Kwikfish are also a deadly lure for those who fish throughout the quiet evening hours.

✧ Jensen Eggs ✧

Impregnated with oil of anise, these salmon-sized plastic egg imitations also make great attractors during turbid water conditions.

The beautiful aspect of artificials is that they have become prolific natural bait alternatives that can often match or exceed the productive capacities of roe. Artificals also reduce the incessant need for eggs which greatly benefits our wild stocks and can save the angler copious amounts of time from having to scrape, preserve, and tie eggs for future outings.

Now that we have discussed some biological aspects of the steelhead and have taken a look at such things as floats, reading water, and which natural and artificial baits to use, it is now time to apply this knowledge to help you connect with the seasonal migrations of our Great Lakes steelhead.

Kwikfish, Jensen Eggs.

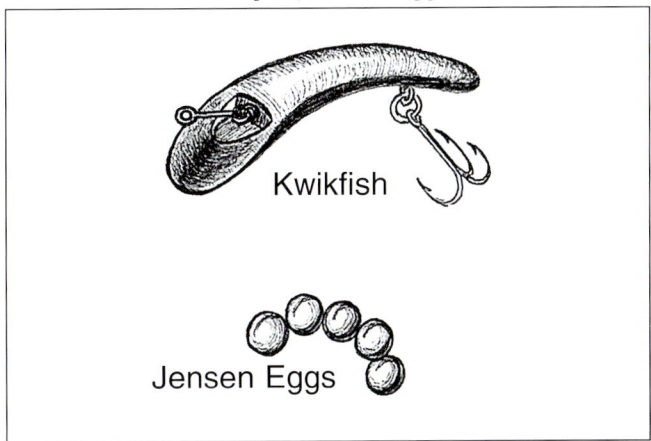

Chapter 5
Autumn Steelhead

After a long lavish summer of chasing down copious amounts of Great Lakes baitfish and gulping down insects from offshore slicks, plump steelhead discover that the decreasing photo period of summer and cooler evening temperatures are summoning them back to rivermouths near the source of their juvenile origins.

In spite of the environmental cues that seem to spark inshore autumnal movements, one must realize that although similar, no two steelhead streams or regions are exactly the same, and as such, no two steelhead populations are either.

Individual steelhead populations have become conditioned to their own regional climate and river regimes, hence, they have developed local adaptations for that region. Therefore, run timing may be moderately different from one region to the next. While environmental cues draw fish to rivermouth areas, local conditions are responsible for the beginning of the run.

As water temperatures drop, opportune environmental conditions now set the stage which will soon allow steelhead to migrate within their preferred environmental parameters. This window of opportunity, as it is often termed, will begin as water temperatures fall into the mid to low 50°F (10-13°C) some time during mid- to late-September. Favorable water temperatures are all that are often needed to start migrations, however, increases in flow through rain events seem to spark

Steelhead populations have become conditioned to their own regional climate and river regimes. Steelhead have therefore developed local adaptations for their specific watersheds. Run timing may be moderately different from one region to the next as a result.

the greatest runs of fish, especially in small to mid-sized tributaries. Steelhead staging off rivermouths though can be easily deterred from migration due to a number of factors such as drought, falling temperatures, and floods, therefore canceling out ideal water temperatures.

Never were these deterring factors more prevalent then during the 2002 autumn steelhead season across Ontario. The drought-like conditions which prevailed throughout the mid 1990s seemed to have peeked in 2001/2002. The trend towards longer, hotter summers with little precipitation has now robbed many mid-sized rivers and creeks of their water supply, and as such, autumn steelhead runs have become seriously interrupted.

Larger rivers, however, with good base flows seem to be less effected by the current drought-like conditions and are often independent of rain events. Their heavy flows, coupled with proper seasonal timing and water temperatures, are often enough to set the migration in motion. Once steelhead do enter tributaries, whether it be temperature or freshet related, their batteries are fully charged and at no other time will you encounter steelhead with such stealth and furry. Their large lake feeding grounds have served them well as they return with enough stored fat and energy reserves to see them through to the end of the spring spawn. Depending on the circumstances, fresh run steelhead can be dispersed throughout many areas within the river shed. Heavy freshets may send them running straight through many low- to mid-river sections and right past anglers. (They take full advantage of the high water conditions while sporadic showers may inspire them to enter the river only to have them drop back down to stage in the lower river pools and estuaries.) Fresh steelhead in close proximity to the lake may in fact still be in their large lake feeding modes as autopsies often reveal *Hexagenia Limbata* nymphs (silt borrowing mayfly nymphs) heavily packed within their stomachs. Perhaps the slow-flowing water in the lower, deeper river regions makes these nymphs such an easy prey item, and as such, the staging steelhead simply can't resist one more feast before heading on to its upstream spawning grounds.

More often than not, small to mid-sized rivers containing sufficient flow and ideal water temperatures of 56-38°F (13-3°C) and lower will have fresh fish trickling in on a regular basis, although, locating them may require some legwork as they can be widely scattered or all grouped up within one or two good pools.

It is not at all uncommon for some of these fish to migrate during the evening hours as night migrations offer steelhead the advantage of discretion. Generally speaking, steelhead will move just before dusk, continue through the night, and will commence toward dawn. Being streamside a half hour or so before the break of dawn may reveal the steelhead's nighttime crusade because downstream water may reveal large wakes of fish on the move.

As dawn approaches watch for fish to hole up in pools, tailouts, blowdowns, and in faster broken water areas behind rocks or obstructions which break the main flow.

In some instances I have witnessed steelhead who seem to play by their own rules, showing little prudence for their safety by challenging shallow silty flats with reckless abandon during periods of broad daylight. The sense of urgency that seems to beckon them upstream during midday certainly goes beyond the realm of what can be considered normal behavior albeit it does exemplify the fact that steelhead have genetically diversified within their own populations and have seemingly developed individual timetables within the window.

As for larger rivers, steelhead may choose to migrate throughout the day as the greater flow in and of itself often provides enough security to allow for continued migration. When rest is required, their holding options are widespread and plentiful simply because of their large environments. Look

When river mouths have sufficient depth, early autumn migration will occur once water temperatures drop to the low to mid 50's (10-13C). Watch for fish to widely scatter throughout the system or be grouped up in pools or tailouts adjacent to shallow riffles or flats.

for them in runs, heads and tailouts, in front and behind rocks and boulders, current seams, along backeddies, pockets, around fallen timber and in deeper riffles with broken water. Each river also seems to possess its own unique combinations of holding water which may make some holding water more favorable than others.

There is no doubt that autumn steelhead runs can take on many forms and as such, can take many anglers by surprise. Those first to arrive in early autumn are the best examples. Generally speaking the diehards are the first to clue in to these early arriving fish trying to keep their early season successes a tightly guarded secret.

Autumn spawning Chinooks have also entered tributaries often weeks in advance of the first steelhead arrivals, and while most anglers are of the mindset that the steelhead have purposefully migrated to feed on loose drifting salmon eggs, the reality is that they have in earnest begun their own migration, but will gladly consume Chinook eggs if the opportunity presents.

Steelhead and Chinooks can often be found within the same stream holding sections, however, they don't seem to get along well as salmon can often be seen chasing the steelhead to the back of pools thus preventing their upstream progress. Suffice it to say that the Chinooks are well aware that steelhead are reaping the rewards of their spawning efforts and are probably agitated by their good fortune.

Although the autumn steelhead run is comprised of many year classes, it is interesting to note that in many cases it is the small "shakers" or "half pounders" that are among the first to arrive. Ironically enough, it was only a few short months ago that these fish were running down to the lake as smolts and now have returned as 14-18 inch (36-46cm) fish. Why these half pounders seem to proceed the larger adults is chiefly unknown. The majority of these shakers return as sexually immature fish. However, studies indicate that indeed there are some precocious males within the population that are able to mate during the spring spawn. Their presence becomes apparent during the spawning activity of the larger adults as they often try to sneak in among the spawning pair only to be chased off by the infuriated male. Their upstream presence isn't without merit since they may indeed mate with larger females if there aren't enough males to go around. If these shakers are showing up as part of your early season catch it's a sure sign that the larger adults are close behind.

Perhaps one of the most crucial bits of information I can provide the reader of this book is where to find early running autumn steelhead within the water column as it differs remarkably from the subtle flows of mid-sized streams to the larger, faster flowing rivers.

It seems that river flow and water temperature play a significant role in where fish choose to locate within the river, as well as where they will choose to situate within the water column. Fresh run steelhead who have just spent the summer feeding and suspending out in the lake also show a preference towards suspending once back in their natal environments. Watch for fish to suspend in water temperatures from 56° down to 38°F (13-3°C). We must also separate the larger flows from the medium-sized streams because fish will be found at different water depths within both water courses.

In larger, faster flowing rivers steelhead will choose to suspend well above the bottom, but at the same time, far enough below the surface as to escape the heavy currents. Try suspending your baits between three and five feet (1-1.5m) below the surface and experiment until you find the strike zone.

Steelhead that have entered the more placid flows of the small to mid-sized rivers and streams do not have to contend with heavy current and can be found suspended well off the bottom to within two or three feet (.6-.9m) below the stream surface.

Anglers with a keen sense of eyesight and good polarized glasses can frequently make out the steelhead's faint ghostly silhouettes as their chrome colored contours closely match those of its suspended depths.

Casting to such fish, however, should be done with slow, methodical movements as not to arise suspicion among the unsuspecting fish. Spooking just one fish will consequently result in spooking them all. Try standing next to large trees to help mask your profile or try kneeling so you are below a fish's cone of vision. Although camouflage clothing isn't standard steelhead garb, I have been wearing it ever since the new realistic patterns started to emerge well over a decade ago. Today I consider camo clothing an integral part of my approach.

Regardless of whether you choose to fish the larger, faster flowing rivers, or the more pristine subtle streams, there is absolutely no denying that prime, fresh run steelhead in either system will be among the easiest fish of the year to catch, and the hardest fighting, since cold temperatures have yet to slow down their metabolic jets, while angling pressure has yet to sequester their spunk.

This is truly prime time for float fishermen.

➷ Presentation, Observation, ➷ and Behaviors

Since we have already said that returning steelhead will strike or feed as a result of opportunity, aggression, or inherent behaviors, it is now time to look more candidly at how we can entice or trigger a response from these eager but often wary sport fish.

Each time an angler delivers his presentation via the float, in reality he is trying to mimic the potential food items that may appear within the constant drift. (The constant drift is merely the downstream transport of aquatic invertebrates and other food items being washed downstream within the current.) However, what most anglers may not be aware of is that steelhead seem to exhibit preferences and may selectively feed on food items within the drift according to abundance, size, shape, color, scent, and bait action. Fish also prefer to feed upon some items according to water temperatures.

I first started making the connection between bait criteria and water temperature several years ago when I began to observe definite patterns between distinct feeding behavior and specific water temperatures.

Not willing to pass off my observations as mere coincidences I began to visit other rivers and also began to make identical observations of steelhead behavior using the same presentations during the same water temperatures, needless to say, the use of a stream thermometer became an integral part of my angling success.

Having catalogued all my observations of steelhead behaviors and bait preferences, I can now take a streamside temperature reading during normal flow and can tell you where the fish are likely to be and what baits they are likely to hit. Knowing where fish will be and what they will hit is all part of the learning curve to continued success. These observations will be revealed to you in the following chapters.

✥ Early Autumn Presentations ✥

As early running steelhead begin to make their presence known throughout the streams in late September, there is no denying that water temperatures in the low to mid 50°F (10-13°C) range has them supercharged and headstrong.

The term "ballistic" comes to mind when trying to detail the fighting capabilities of fresh-run autumn chrome steelhead. Most times, all the angler can do is hold on and question whether or not he should push up to heavier pound leaders and mainline. No doubt hooked fish take little time in reacquainting themselves with every stick, twig, or overhanging branch in the swim, and if they can't find a way to snap you off below the surface, then they will surely try to above it with head shaking, cart wheeling leaps, often one after another, throw in a double tale slap to boot, and if he hasn't wrapped up and snapped the line by now, you may just have a shot at landing one. That is if it doesn't decide to bolt when you try and beach it in the shallows. With everything somewhat under control you bend down with your hemostats and twist the hook out of its mouth, but before you can standup again the fish has bee-lined it back into the place you hooked it from. Such are the ways of the autumn steelhead.

As mentioned earlier in this section, autumn run steelhead have entered rivers and streams to embark on their own spawning crusades and not for the sole purposes of feeding on salmon eggs, however, you would be a little hard pressed to prove that theory judging by the amount of steelhead that we catch each autumn season using roe.

At this time of year, steelhead seem to show a distinct preference for certain roe bag colors. One of the many behavioral observations I have made over my two decades of pursuing Great Lakes steelhead is that steelhead show a distinct predisposition for the color pink during the early to mid phases of their autumn migrations. Mid-September through early November is when this color seems to peak.

Ironically enough, pink is also one of the most prominent colors used on Pacific Northwest steelhead which only seems to prove that Great Lakes steelhead are not that far removed from their "home turf" and that they have still maintained their habitual tenacity.

I first began to clue into the merits of pink many years ago as a few friends and I were drifting natural-colored sacs to low clear-water fish with no results. Changing to pink, as a last resort, yielded me the only fish in the pool at which time it became inherently clear that steelhead had a preference. It was at this

Early running autumn steelhead find roe presentations hard to resist.

time that the pink pattern seemed to follow suit in subsequent experiments for low clear-water steelhead in the years that followed.

To show you the confidence I have in pink it is now, and has been for years, the only color I carry for early season successes. In fact if you were to ever sneak a peak at my roe container (you'd better be quick) you would soon realize that I hold this color in very high regard. Regardless of where you fish across the Great Lakes, try pink first as it has worked for me wherever I have fished.

Although pink seems to be the magic color for early season, one must also consider that angling pressure is at an all-time high these days as the popularity of steelheading has seemingly soared. When you combine angling pressure, and high traffic areas with easy access and critically low water then it becomes quite evident that fish will be off the bite to more popular baits. If you are extremely limited as to your options, try using some of the small jigs or small live worms that we discussed in the bait sections. My honest advice is to look for fresh unmolested eager fish. This might mean having to fish the rivermouth and harbor areas until more favorable stream conditions exist.

➷ Rivermouths and Piers ✧

If you recall the nightmarish droughts that plagued the 2002 autumn steelhead season then you remember that most Great Lakes areas with wild runs of steelhead were virtually void of fish. Those that adapted and knew where to look made out fine, while those that waited for rains had a long depressing wait. The best fishing near my home waters meant having to remove the float in place of an egg sinker and while this book is mainly about float fishing we must consider that today's steelheader absolutely has to adapt or they are going to be spending a lot more time at home watching fishing on T.V. and since I'd rather have a rod in my hand over the remote I spent a great deal of the autumn in pursuit of rivermouth rainbows.

If the truth be known, I rather enjoy fishing the rivermouth and piers as the same excitement can be had from watching a bouncing rod tip as can be had by watching your float. Either way, it is quite an adrenaline rush when a head shaking steelhead decides to inhale your offering.

It seems as though staging steelhead are also keen on the color pink as it appears to be the predominate color in the lake as well. Try adding peach Styrofoam floaters to accent the overall color. Another popular color seems to be chartreuse roe bags with white contrasting Styrofoam floaters and its reverse, white with chartreuse floaters. Some days one color will perform better than the other. Why this happens only the fish truly know.

Some innovative anglers often include small bits of marshmallows in with their roe claiming that the added sugar frequently attracts fish while others use the powerful scent of a Jensen egg threaded on their line above the hook for the same purpose.

Having used all of these rivermouth tactics at one time or another I have concluded that they work no better or worse than just a plain, ordinary floating roe sac. What will make a big difference is the size of your roe sac offering.

Most anglers I see use roe sacs that are way to small. Don't be afraid to use large sacs, the size of a quarter or slightly larger, as these steelhead are far from being hook shy. As part of their aggressive nature, rivermouth steelhead do have a tendency to take these suspended roe sacs quite deep so I urge you to keep a close eye on your rod tips and strike quickly once fish hit to avoid deeply hooking and possibly injuring fish.

Heavy 1 oz. egg sinkers and large floating roe sacs are some of the keys to surf side success. Scott Sampson quickly displays the merits of fishing the wind blown surf.

Last minute decisions to fish rivermouths by anglers having no luck upstream can try fishing their sacs straight on the bottom as this often works, however, they may want to invest in a handful of brightly colored buoyant corkies to keep in their vest when forced there in the future.

To get baits far offshore, try using heavier egg sinkers in the one-ounce category. Not only do they cast further but they are also heavy enough to stay put when heavy winds start whipping the lake around. Keep baits to within 12-18 inches (30-43 cm) off of bottom. Given the fact that rivermouth steelhead will be in their best shape of the entire year it goes without saying that reels should be filled to the rim as long runs in vast open lakes are the norm. You may even want to step up your line test since these fish are extremely aggressive and are far from being line shy.

On one occasion last season (2002) I had a steelhead snap me off and, while re-rigging, my partner ended up hooking the exact same fish as my roe bag and leader were still intact. Needless to say, despite being hooked only seconds beforehand this fish still maintained its aggressive behavior and paid little attention to the other lines around it.

For the most part, eight pound (3.7kg) mainline should suit the rivermouth steelheader but one thing that became apparent to me rather quickly was that fluorocarbon leaders for this style of fishing are absolutely useless as their low stretch characteristic often resulted in lost fish during long distance hooksets. As we have already noted, fish are aggressive anyway so simply stick to regular mono lines for your leaders.

Perhaps the greatest misconception about fishing off of rivermouths is that steelhead will stage directly in front of the rivermouth where the current is spilling far out into the lake. While this is a good general starting point, fish often locate to either side of where the lake and river waters mix far down the shoreline of the actual rivermouth. Graphing the contours of your local rivermouths during a summer boat trip may well be worth the effort in terms of your autumn success. Look for any type of holding structure from fast drop-offs, to rock or boulder outcrops, to sunken logs, or old sunken docks within your casting distance from shore.

For those without a boat, you may unveil the best rivermouth locations by fishing along the shore in intervals making mental notes of where your best successes have come from. Of course there's always the easy way out and that is to watch where the locals are fishing doing a little detective work can often pay huge dividends. Connecting with Great Lakes steelhead within rivermouth regions can often be a hit or miss endeavor as the fishing can be fast and furious one day, and then with a shift in the wind, totally dead the next.

I have had days where the fish were so abundant that no sooner had I casted out and wadded back to shore another fish would hit just as I set the rod back in the rod stand, only to return the next day without so much as a sniff or a bump from a steelhead.

The sudden and abrupt turnaround can often be attributed to shifts in wind direction as fish will follow their preferred water temperatures once they are bounced around the lake.

Generally speaking, onshore winds pushing in warmer lake water appear to be the trigger responsible for coaxing large inshore movements of fish. Conversely, offshore winds have the opposite effect and send fish further out into the lake.

Oddly enough, it is the small 14- to 18-inch (36-46 cm) shakers who make the first appearance off the rivermouths once early evening onshore winds first start to set up. Although bothersome, hooking these small silvery shakers is an extremely good sign that the rivermouth and pier fishermen need to clue into for it undoubtedly means that the larger adults will be in the immediate vicinity by the following morning.

As onshore waves intensify overnight, steelhead are drawn closer to near shore areas and are easily taken by the plunkers who have clued into steelheads' habitual rivermouth patterns.

Some of my most memorable rivermouth outings have taken place during these intense onshore waves, especially, the kind that seem to body slam you as you try and jump out of their way. I absolutely love fishing under such harsh and abrupt weather scenarios not because I am a deranged steelheader but because it really seems to set steelhead activity into high gear.

Fishing under these harsh conditions still means having to walk out into the lake for maximum casting distance, but never travel further than your comfort zone allows. Keep in mind that it will be more difficult to walk back to shore than it is to wade into the pounding surf as water pilling onshore makes its way back out into the lake.

While walking out into the surf, leave your vest onshore but bring your roe supply as it will come in handy in case the sac you are using tears off during a heaving cast. Watch for steelhead action to start dying off once inshore waves become so heavy that they stir up the sediments and dirty the lake shores. At this point, fish will seek out cleaner water beyond casting range.

Piers and Breakwalls

Rivers containing deep harbor areas are often some of the first locations to be visited by returning steelhead. Here fish will often move in and out between the deep harbor waters and the deeper lake water as they try to decide whether or not conditions are favorable for migration.

Generally speaking, fish will move into these harbor areas throughout the overnight periods during onshore winds, however, since the water is sufficiently deep they will also traverse during calmer conditions as well.

More often than not, float fishermen fishing from piers and breakwalls at first light stand a pretty good chance at connecting with these fish as they start to make tacks back to the deeper waters of the lake with the rising sun.

Switching from inner harbor floats to large lake egg sinkers as the sun climbs higher should put you back on top of the fish—especially during choppy water.

Wind directions, such as those in natural rivermouths, will once again dictate fish location, however, things take on a little different shape because of the presence of the piers and breakwalls. Heavy winds will usually push fish to the opposite side of the breakwall where calmer waters will prevail. For instance, gusty winds kicking up heavy lake swells from the west will generally push fish behind the calmer sheltering waters of the east breakwall as the water's energy dissipates after crashing into the inner harbor walls. The opposite will occur in an east wind as fish will reside behind the west breakwall. Steelhead will often cruise the edge of the rough and calm waters in search of prey and this is where you should begin your pursuit. Don't forget your long handled nets as they are an absolute must for the breakwall bunch especially during days of drought and low lake levels.

Despite the fact that piers and breakwalls are often productive pieces of fish catching real estate, I still prefer the solitude and tranquillity of natural rivermouths as they are generally far less crowded and provide a greater sense of fulfillment upon landing a fish within their oftentimes temperamental environments.

➔ Freshets, Turbid Water, ← and Behavior

Given that the proper seasonal timing and water temperatures are paramount for opening the seasonal migration window, it is often the freshets that are most responsible for drawing the greatest numbers of migrating fish upstream.

Whether in the form of runoff from snow melt, or regional rainfall, freshets will inevitably raise water levels, increase flows, and reduce visibility by various degrees within the stream environment. The way in which we interpret how steelhead will react to these degrees will unquestionably lead us to more fish.

Substantial rain events no doubt spark new life into the steelhead who in all likelihood have been eagerly staging in lower pools, estuaries, and rivermouth regions for weeks. The increased flows and

Deep harbor areas and piers are often the first to attract fresh autumn steelhead. Watch for fresh fish to sniff around piers and breakwalls during onshore winds or during calm conditions during overnight, morning or evening periods.

During high turbid water situations, fish migrate in the slower, shallower water margins. Use large gaudy multicolored visual presentations such as a Gooey Bob and a roe sac with discarded roe sac material for added eye appeal.

noticeably reduced visibility have finally afforded these fish the freedom of migration.

Fishing for steelhead during these adverse situations can be a rather challenging endeavor as the conditions are often intimidating and angler confidence seems to decrease with every inch of reduced visibility. However, all is not lost and good fishing opportunities often exist provided the angler has at least four inches of water visibility to work with and has some fundamental knowledge of high-water fish behavior.

Let's take a closer look.

Generally speaking, steelhead migrating during high turbid water conditions will exhibit totally different behaviors as compared to when the rivers were low and clear.

With the abundant water volume that exists, steelhead can easily glide upstream within the slack water, tight to shore, or in slack water areas out from the main flow. Here, fish are totally out of the main current and can easily access upstream water virtually undetected. The water throughout these near shore sections is also visibly cleaner than the main flow which will be a big plus in terms of helping the fish to find your presentation. Another way of looking at it is to fish those areas that you would never normally consider fishing during low, clear water.

It should be noted that although we can find cooperative fish during these adverse water conditions, one must learn to differentiate between holding and moving fish as one has a tendency to feed while the other may not.

For the most part, fish that are in transit are primarily focused on migration and not on feeding, therefore, if you are fishing in an area where fish are motoring right past you, then the odds are against you hooking any of them.

Fish may move upstream and bypass several good areas until they finally decide to pause and rest. Observe the wakes these fish make as they move upstream and watch for where they stop, in all likelihood they will meet up with other fish that have selected a suitable holding area. It is in these holding areas that fish are more willing to accept a drifted offering.

Since we are dealing with drastic water conditions we must combat them with drastic measures. Given a minimum visibility of around four inches (10cm) this calls for amplified baits. For maximum visibility I started experimenting with amplified or large baits and attractors quite extensively in the early 1990s simply because my hometown creek was infamous for staying very dirty during the spring thaw and remained that way through the peak of the spring steelhead runs. Fishing throughout the dirty water periods has revealed some very interesting facts about what baits fish were likely to hit during periods of reduced visibility. Although my dirty water cocktail presentations have gone through many changes over the years, here are the two which I primarily use now. First off, thread a chartreuse Jensen egg onto your leader. Then add a bead to prevent it from slipping back down onto the hook. Tie on a #8 or #10 Daiichi hook and to this thread on a quarter size pink roe bag. Once this is done, tear open a used roe bag or two (preferable chartreuse or orange) and then pierce them back onto your hook so that they hang down beneath your roe sac. This presentation won me the 1996 Bowmanville Creek live release steelhead tournament that was held during some of the dirtiest water conditions I've ever fished.

My updated version of this nowadays is to simply use a pearl/pink gooey bob and bead with a large chartreuse roe bag along with a used piece of roe bag material (with or without Jensen egg). The important thing to remember is to try and use a variety of fluorescent colors to help create a clown-colored neon presentation. I especially like to use these dirty water presentations during sunny days as the fluorescent colors seem to become highlighted within the stained water.

So what are these dirty water cocktails suppose to represent? My only guess would be a large visual feeding opportunity. Try one of these clown-colored cocktails in close to shore the next time your regional waters are running high and turbid. They should improve your success and build you confidence for future dirty water outings.

➤ Mid to Late Autumn ➤

Given that some early runs of steelhead have already progressed upstream throughout the September and October periods, it seems as though the best steelheading is still yet to come as November and December are customarily considered to be prime steelhead months.

By now the Chinook salmon that have proceeded the early steelhead runs weeks prior have thinned out considerably. Having seeded their genetic blueprints safely within the gravel riffles, their large carcasses now adorn the streambanks and shallows. Their passing though, need not be viewed as a waste because the nutrients they have carried with them back from the large lakes will now feed the yearling trout and promote the growth of algae which in turn will feed small invertebrates and so on thus linking together the communities within the aquatic food chain. Suffice it to say, in nature, nothing goes to waste.

Yearling steelhead it seems, often reap the immediate rewards of these rotting carcasses as fair numbers of emerging blow fly larvae no doubt loose their footing and become swept up in the currents providing these parr with a few extra calories to help see them through the cold months ahead.

Anglers using wax worms as bait throughout the year may now see a biological connection as to why these baits work so well since they closely resemble both blow fly and caddis larvae.

Since we are speaking of early to mid-November, your best color choice may still be pink, however, for some reason I have found that this is also the time when steelhead tend to focus more of their attention on to chartreuse. Try using chartreuse for both clear and stained flows and use less pink as the season progresses. Other productive color choices include pale yellow, and white but for the most part you can't go wrong with chartreuse.

While we are still on the topic of roe use, we also need to address how its effectiveness may become comprised as autumn progresses. Generally speaking, roe can become an overused bait choice especially as steelhead begin to hold in pool areas for longer periods of time during colder water transitions. Here, most of them will have been caught and released and may subsequently reject further roe presentations. These unruly fish may be taken again during first light situations once their guard is down but for the most part, heavy angling pressure in popular locations will turn these fish off entirely. Now fishing for them with roe simply becomes an exercise in casting. Suffice it to say that fish do not become less hungry during mid to late autumn they just become more educated. Roe may also become a "take it or leave it" type of bait as the season progresses and the cold water period becomes more prevalent. It seems that lowering water temperatures not only lower steelheads' metabolism but it also seems to alter their feeding behaviors. Keep this fact in the front of your mind because it is paramount and from this point forward we will address when alternative baits will work best and at which temperatures.

Of course a substantial late autumn freshet that stains the flow will start pushing these fish and fresh arrivals upstream, at which time they will let down their guard and start hitting roe again as it remains rather distinguishable throughout the stained flows. It should be noted, however, that each situation may be a little different and it will be up to the steelheader to identify what behavior the steelhead will exhibit given current conditions.

➢ Decreasing Temperatures, ➣ a Key to Behavior

Perhaps the most crucial element that will dictate steelhead behavior throughout the late autumn and winter period is the declining water temperatures. Many years ago I began to make a correlation between water temperatures, steelhead locations, and their bait preferences after my success rate with roe and everyone else's for that matter seemed to taper off by mid to late November. Intrigued by our lack of success I began to explore other bait prospects and soon began to make great strides in unwrapping the mysterious behaviors of our cold water steelhead. The one reoccurring constant that I did peg down to almost a science was the fact that steelhead seem to prefer certain bait sizes and types based upon the temperature of their environment.

Although that seemed pretty cut and dry I also noticed that steelhead often needed to acclimate to the water temperatures as they periodically changed from day to day. Let's take a closer look.

Judging from my temperature readings taken over many steelhead seasons it appears steelhead behavior takes a turn when water temperatures dip to 41°F (5°C). At this temperature a steelhead's metabolism, for some unknown reason, now allows it to seek out larger baits and wobbling lures which would otherwise trigger flight response in mid-sized streams. One lure is the

Water temperatures play a major role in steelhead feeding behavior. Once temperatures drop to the 41F (5C) range steelhead appear more inclined to chase larger lures such as wobbling Kwikfish. Increases in temperature such as those found throughout spring have just the opposite effect and activate the fishes flight response.

Kwikfish. I am sure you are all familiar with this wobbling banana bait and I must say that I have learned a great deal about steelhead behavior from their use. Again, I know at this point you must be saying that this book is supposed to be about float fishing and it is for the most part. However, when we speak in terms of a successful outing, the angler must learn to adapt to the whims of the steelhead, otherwise he goes fishless. Besides, you can always trot a Kwikfish beneath a float or keep it stationary as I have often done with ultimate results. Going back to our 41°F (5°C) theory I also came to the conclusion that these lures also worked slightly outside of this temperature range when water temperatures rose to 43-46°F (6-8°C) range but only until the steelhead's metabolism has a chance to acclimate to the new water temperatures, at which point the steelhead sometimes follow the bait or was afraid of it until the temperatures leveled back out to the 41°F (5°C) mark. It seems that these wobbling plugs produced best between 41°F (5°C) down to 36°F (2°C) range then the fish were usually turned off, not willing to chase it in the cold water again until they once more acclimated to the decreasing water temperatures.

The temperature Kwikfish data that I have accumulated over the years has paid off handsomely, especially during periods of low water and high angling pressure. Going back to the autumn 2000 season, I vividly remember arriving at the local river a half hour before sun up only to find a parking lot full of anglers hastily making their way down to the river. Not wanting to fall behind, I grabbed my rod and off I went . I became discouraged as a couple of anglers deemed it necessary to quicken their pace and pass me. Looking up and down the river every single pool, nook, and cranny had a fisherman in it so I decided to leave and come back in the afternoon as I already knew what the steelhead were going to take in the 41°F (5°C) water. Upon my return, there were only a couple of locals left working their way out. They claimed the fishing earlier in the morning was less than ideal which put a huge smile on my face, for now I had both the river and the fish to myself. The long and short of it was that I ended up going 8 for 11 in 41°F (5°C) water temperatures with Kwikfish, while all the roe chuggers had left early because they hadn't clued in to what the steelhead were willing to hit.

In another instance I came upon a hole that required the use of a Kwikfish, however, the hole was occupied by an older gentleman and his grandkids. I fished the back of the hole, patiently all the while eyeing a beautiful piece of shelf ice that they had totally ignored. They finally left and I made my way to the top of the ice shelf and trotted a Kwikfish beneath a float along the edge of the ice. Holding the float stationary for no more than a minute produced a rather large, robust male in the high teens. It seems to me that in both scenarios these anglers were unaware of the habitual tendencies of steelhead in relation to cooling water temperatures and therefore left the stream without having made the connection. Those wishing to try Kwikfish during decreasing temperatures should try K-5 through K-8 sizes in black colors.

Kwikfish are not the only bait that will work during these decreasing water temperatures as I also have come to rely heavily on simple black steelhead jigs. Fish them under a float and twitch the float every so often to impart movement which will suggest life within the bait. Perhaps it is the movement with both of these baits which fish find so appealing.

✦ Night Fishing ✦

Anglers who may be unable to fish during autumn daylight periods, or who just generally dislike fishing with the masses, can consider getting their steelhead fix during overnight periods.

Holdover steelhead often let their guard down during late-evening hours, especially if they see moderate angling pressure throughout the day.

Regardless of whether you choose to drift a night-time presentation beneath a float, fish bottom or toss Kwikfish through slow flows, steelhead have no problem locating night time presentations.

CHAPTER 5: AUTUMN STEELHEAD | 49

In other scenarios, fish residing in downstream sections may start pool hopping to new upstream holding areas while fresh fish may be coming in from the lake. In any event, it soon becomes apparent that fish activity certainly picks up throughout the overnight hours.

Having made some extensive night shift excursions over the years I can certainly tell you that steelhead are in no way disadvantaged at night and can easily sniff out a variety of prey items and baits without discretion.

In fact, their nighttime feeding forays may often coincide with the stream's behavioral drift. The behavioral drift is simply a nocturnal life strategy used by some aquatic invertebrates to search out new territories. Steelhead may feed on these drifting invertebrates and the small baitfish who chase them.

This may explain why plain black marabou steelhead jigs suspended under a float during the nighttime hours have worked so well for me during some of my late night shift excursions.

Kwikfish throughout the 41°F (5°C) water temperatures have also served me well during the witching hours as their slow, enticing side-to-side movements can provoke strikes from even the most wary steelhead. Fish the K5 to K8 models with a super slow retrieve in order to give steelhead ample time to hunt them down. To get baits down into the strike zone quicker, simply add some split shot to within eight inches (20cm) of the bait.

Other productive baits that I have had success with under the float are glow-in-the-dark tube jigs though they do not seem to glow for more than a couple of drifts. Keep a flashlight close at hand and keep zapping these baits because they can be super productive. Of course roe works great under a float or strictly on bottom. Try tying larger bags for this type of fishing and occasionally reel back in to squeeze the eggs to re-start the milking action. Steelhead will no doubt pick up this vapor trail and zero in on your bait.

When the night shift beacon's, be sure to focus most of your efforts throughout the slow-moving pool areas and make sure you are familiar with your immediate surroundings.

Float fishing darkened pools throughout the calm evening hours with only a night stick to focus on seems to spark added anticipation for the night shift angler. Watching the faint night stick suddenly sink into the clear depths of a dark pool, or feeling that subtle take while pulling a slow-moving plug, is an adrenaline rush that for some is unparalleled to that of day fishing.

Perhaps the darkened environment adds to the mystique of the night fishing experience. In any event, veteran night owls know that they may have to work a little harder for their fish, but in the long run, for them, that is what makes landing one a little more eventful.

➸ Late Autumn, Early Winter ᚛

As water temperatures dip down to the 36-37°F (2-3°C) range, and late fall transforms into early winter, steelhead behavior changes once again. Fish can now be found in close proximity to the bottom of selected wintering pools in both large and mid-sized streams alike. If you recall, back in our float chapter, I gave a brief description on how you can easily find out where the fish are simply by attaching a homemade plumb bomb to your hook, adjusting your float until it sits just under the surface. I can't begin to explain how many times I have watched anglers fish wintering pools with their presentation only suspended at half the depth that they needed to be at. The moral to the steelhead story at this time of year is simple: Find the bottom and there you will find fish.

Try pearl colored tube jigs under a float as temperatures begin to hover around 36-37°F (2-3°C). Twitch them on occasion, try to trigger a strike if fish are overly lethargic. Fish will frequently switch back and forth from tube jigs to marabou so keep both types with you at all times.

➸ Trophy Steelhead ᚛

Depending on the type of year that presents itself, and the subsequent temperature, the late autumn/early winter angler may continue to pursue steelies in and around forming river slush and shelf ice, however, there may not be as many fish around as most of the earlier fish have already made the push further upstream. The vacant pools and their depths will now be visited by what might very well be the largest steelhead of the autumn run.

For some unknown reason, the largest of the large, those 20-25 pound (9-11kg) plus steelhead seem to begin their upstream journey toward the end of the autumn season. Perhaps they are aware of the ice canopy that will soon cover the waterways which will afford them added security as they push upstream.

It has always been my experience that these true Great Lakes trophies don't seem to run with the pack, in fact, they appear to find solace in their own company.

Having totaled three of these elusive Great Lakes giants, and a few more that have made the upper teens (all were released), I can honestly say that each of these males was a true loaner as no other fish were caught before or after them within their respective pools.

Their fighting qualities, on the other hand, like most fish in 33°F (.5°C) water, leaves a lot to be desired.

Setting the hook on these Great Lakes behemoths will at first lead you to believe that you have hooked bottom, and just when you contemplate having to snap off and retie, they give their first lazy head shake. Their delayed reaction can no doubt be attributed to the cold water and the fact that our tiny hooks have little impact on their rather large, hard bony mouths.

Their dour fighting abilities can often be comparable to a bear slowly beginning to awaken after a long, cold, winter hibernation. To say that they lack theatrics would be an understatement. However, this is to be expected since these fish really are enduring possibly the coldest climates of their introduced range. Generally speaking, hooking one no doubt will be the highlight of your angling forays. Expect some haphazard runs, some bull dogging for bottom, and a lot of slow, methodical head shakes. And watch for sharp shelves of ice if it is around as this seems to be their "go to" move when all other attempts fail. Of course if temperatures are warmer you can expect to have your hands full.

As noted earlier, in Chapter Two, these Great Lakes trophies generally make up less than one percent of the total steelhead population and to keep one would surely do an injustice to the gene pool. So please, take some pictures and some measurements, then set them free so they may pass along those genes for large growth and longevity to the next generation.

Trophy steelhead over the 20lb mark are few and far between. They appear to find solace in their own company as they are often the lone occupant of a pool. Here the author displays a 35.5 x 23.25 or 24lb male caught during a miserable rainy late December morning. No fish were caught in the pool before or after this colossal fish which helps to validate their solitary behaviors.

Chapter 6
Winter Steelhead

When one conjectures up images of winter across the vast expanses of the mighty Great Lakes, they are often quick to surmise that the region is bound by mass accumulations of snowfall, howling cold Arctic winds, and bone chilling below freezing temperatures.

While this is a pretty fair assessment of our regional weather scenario, some of our winters have failed to live up to their harsh and acquired reputations.

Some rogue winter steelhead play by their own rules and migrate despite cold temperatures. Migration in the dead of winter is unusual although Great Lakes steelhead are often full of surprises.

The relatively mild nature of some of the lower Great Lakes winters of late has afforded anglers in many regions extended fishing opportunities as the mild temperatures have left many river corridors open and only partially ice covered. In some instances, such as during the winter of 2002, river ice was virtually non-existent as the winter was considered to be the warmest winter since records have been kept.

Each winter though, seems to bring with it a different set of weather variables and being the adaptable creatures that they are, steelhead have learned to adjust to these weather variances, making full use of any migration opportunities that may present themselves.

During relatively mild types of winters with little ice, the migration window can remain open for longer periods of time, and fish can continue upstream at will, especially when assisted by mild winter rains or snow melt.

The earliest migrations I have ever encountered were in January of 2002 as mild temperatures and moderate rains activated a mix of fresh and over wintering fish which were quick on the move. Before long they were jumping low, overhead lamprey barriers in 34°F (1.5°C) water temperatures. On the contrary, typical cold winter weather will have over wintering river steelhead behaving quite differently. It seems that most of these holdover steelhead remain rather docile and dormant throughout the coldest periods until a warming trend, or increases in flow, reactivate their migrations.

It should be noted, however, that not all steelhead are cut from the same cloth and despite a cold winter there always seems to be those few fresh chromers that manage to sneak upstream under the ice from the lake. I have hooked into a few of these early chrome migrants over the years, one of which was during a mid-January afternoon in a river bend that only had about three feet (.9m) of open water alongside an ice shelf.

My winter presentation proved worthy of a takedown and after some fancy rod maneuvering around the jagged ice edge, I was able to coax a beautiful chrome-colored hen into shore. The fish was so fresh, I wondered if it hadn't arrived in the pool only minutes before I caught it. These winter migrants, however, are far and few between.

Rivermouth regions, which contain deep harbor areas, are also great mid- to late-winter steelhead haunts since it is here that steelhead seem to mill around the most, making back and forth pilgrimages from the large lake to the harbor and back again. Generally speaking, these fish will migrate upstream until they come to the first shallow water section where they will slowly drift back down and eventually end up throughout the depths between the estuary and the lake. This in and out behavior is especially characteristic toward the latter part of February into March as maturing gonads have them eager to begin the run. Steelheaders should focus their efforts around the heavy onshore wind periods as incoming waves from the lake will break up any inner harbor ice giving them access to over wintering and cruising steelhead. Some of my most memorable harbor fishing has taken place under such conditions, especially within the back and forth ice flows of estuaries where fresh and staging steelhead like to group.

✦ Winter Feeding and Tactics ✦

Despite frigid winter water temperatures and a reduced metabolism, steelhead will continue to feed throughout the winter period albeit their opportunities may not be as plentiful as they were earlier in the year.

Now steelhead will nourish themselves by tapping into their stored fat reserves and by accosting small invertebrates.

Quite frankly, steelhead can become easy targets for attentive anglers keeping a vigilant watch on opening stream stretches during unstable winter weather or during January thaws. Locating partially open water may make for some awkward fishing at times, however, fish generally hit baits as soon as they are presented. Their quick response times no doubt represents limited feeding opportunities.

Despite what some may suggest about winter steelhead fishing, do not wait to fish midday periods in hopes of slight increases in water temperature to help activate fish. Steelhead will often hit during first light situations in lieu of the slightly cooler temperature. Waiting to fish midday periods may mean you have waited too long, especially in popular areas that sustain heavy angling pressure.

During these mid-winter thaw scenarios watch for fair numbers of fish that have begun moving upstream to accumulate in slow holdover pool areas in-between evening migrations. Shallow riffles spilling into such pools will often deter fish from further migration, so please practice catch-and-release measures when fishing under these types of circumstances.

In other scenarios, watch for fish to hopscotch from pool to pool when moderate flow and depths permit, again watch for fair numbers to accumulate in certain stream stretches.

Since the flow regime may differ from one pool to the next, look for steelhead to gravitate towards the slowest flow. Try the still pocket water at the heads of pools (when they exist), as well as back eddies, and the slow-flowing seams that traverse alongside the main flow. Fish the slowest, deepest pool sections, top to bottom, if no other holding extras are present.

I can't begin to tell you how many times throughout mild winters or January thaws that I have checked a river stretch on a hunch only to find the stretch was open without any boot prints around to suggest it had yet to be fished. Fishing these areas has produced single-fish days followed by multiple hook-ups on subsequent outings as the mild spell inevitably activated upstream movements that grouped fish in some deeper pools.

It should be noted though that with the return of colder temperatures or during periods of heavy

Keep a vigilant watch over local streams during unstable winters and January thaws. If river sections open steelhead will often take the first feeding opportunity they are presented with. Fish the slowest, deepest water nearby.

CHAPTER 6: WINTER STEELHEAD | 53

angling pressure, groups of steelhead may often make an about face and can begin to head back downstream to quieter, undisturbed lower river holding pools, the estuary, and the lake itself.

I have come across this situation on a number of occasions as well.

Case in point: On some mid-sized streams that we fish, we have watched the fishing go from great to poor (angling pressure) in certain regions in short periods of time.

Having done some leg work we subsequently located good numbers once again in the lower river regions that we had previously fished without any hook-ups. To suggest that these lower river fish may have been fresh migrants is debatable, though our experiences have made us believe that these fish were on their way back down to the estuary.

Unfortunately for the angler, mid-winter thaws usually do not last long and it often seems that just as quickly as the river stretches open up, they refreeze.

These up and down winter weather patterns will thaw and refreeze the river several times throughout an unstable winter, and the brief fishing window they provide can spell prime time fishing for the watchful steelheader.

→ Thinking Outside the Box ←

Since steelhead remain opportunistic in their feeding behavior throughout the winter period, they are easily caught using a variety of float fishing presentations. However, anglers need to think in terms of the big picture when theorizing about bait choices and fish behavior. Fresh migrating fish that have yet to be caught and educated will often accept roe presentations, but not always. On the other hand, over wintering fish that have been caught and released may not be as readily accepting of roe.

But again, roe with its renowned reputation as the ultimate steelhead bait has taken center stage as the preferred bait of choice with winter steelheaders, however, the overconfidence that these anglers have in this bait often seriously interferes with their winter steelhead success.

Don't get me wrong. I have successfully taken steelhead while using roe on mid-winter steelhead myself, but after many, many winters of streamside experimentation and learning to think outside of the box, I have concluded that in most cases nothing will consistently put you on to more open water winter steelhead than the simple steelhead jig.

I can write this with the greatest confidence simply because I have lived it season after season, winter after winter. In fact, during the 2001 winter season I used homemade marabou jigs during those intermittent open water periods to connect with 90 percent of my winter thaw steelhead. I gained so much confidence in their use that roe no longer became an integral part of my winter angling arsenal and it stayed in the freezer. Gaining this knowledge has also led me to release more fish (not that I kept many anyhow) as my need for roe dropped by ninety percent.

Today, given proper water conditions, I fish with as much confidence with jigs as most steelheaders do with the roe presentations. Having experimented with them during a quick melt or rain, I can also relate that they became no less effective throughout moderately stained flows.

So the question begs, why then do jigs and nymphs often perform so much better than the standard roe presentation during cold water periods? One possible explanation could suggest that roe became less of a prominent food source throughout the winter period, while another theory may suggest that returning holdover steelhead no doubt recall the early emergence of winter invertebrates which they fed upon as juvenile fish.

Some invertebrates, such as the prolific midge, begin to emerge as early as January through cracks in the ice while others, like the tiny winter black stonefly (# 18 to 20), and the larger early black stonefly (# 10 to 14) hatch from January until April.

Steelhead will readily intercept these food sources as they leave stream bottoms on their ascent towards the surface (midges) and towards streambanks (stoneflies).

Bead-head jigflies, marabou jigs and bead-head nymphs of various color and sizes can represent a multitude of these and other naturally occurring food items. Tied on large number two jig hooks, black marabou jigs are suggestive of large *Pteronarcys* stonefly nymphs which are real brutes measuring in at one and a half to two inches in length. Having a three-year life cycle throughout most streams of the Great Lakes they can be tied on numerous hook sizes to represent each life stage. Tied on smaller sized jig hooks they may also be suggestive of the early black stones. Switching to lighter tan or cream colored jigs can often imitate *Hexagenia* or burrowing mayfly nymphs.

Generally speaking, try number six sized jigs but don't be afraid to experiment with larger sizes as fish often prefer them in cold water due to their lowered metabolisms.

Switching from feathers to plastics, tube jigs with their abundant color patterns also make excellent winter baits. They also make great switch over baits in areas sustaining heavy fishing pressure or for just finicky steelhead in general. On more than a few occasions I have had finicky steelhead bump a bait with lightening speed and just as quickly spit out the offering. This is a sure sign of an eager but cautious fish that may have been stung or caught and released earlier. Quite often taking off the "bumped bait" and switching it with an alternate, such as marabou for a tube or vice versa, has often led to my connecting with hesitant fish almost instantaneously. Rest the area then switch baits next time this happens to you. To say that jigs are useful baits to connect with Great Lakes winter steelhead would be a definite understatement. Try twitching some under your float if conditions permit next winter and you may find yourself leaving the roe bags at home more often.

❖ Perils of Winter Fishing ❖

Anglers arriving streamside in the a.m. may be faced with less than ideal water conditions as the colder overnight temperatures may produce heavy mounds of flowing stream slush which never seems to leave enough open water for a fluent drift. Even retrieving line can be a chore as cold air and water temperatures conspire by slushing up long drifts of line and freezing up rod guides. While there isn't much you can do about line slush, other then hit the coffee shop, there is something you can do to help offset the accumulation of guide ice and prolong the time you need to spend physically removing it. Having tried Vaseline and commercial fishing pastes that claim to help alleviate guide ice, I was unsatisfied with the minimal results and decided to take the advice of a seasoned fishing acquaintance who introduced me to a brand of fishing guides that he had built onto his rods years ago. These guides were unlike any other guide that I was familiar with since they contained no ceramic insert whatsoever, but rather, they had just a plain metal appearance. They go under the brand name of Pucci Guides and although they do not totally eliminate guide ice, they sure do a better job than Vaseline or commercial fishing pastes.

I have a rod with Pucci guides that I have built specifically for winter river fishing and I have used it for years. Steelheaders wanting to build a winter rod, or are having one built for them, should also consider using larger than normal rod guides from the rod tip, and back at least two guides, as it is here that all of your icing troubles are confined. Talk to a rod builder as he will know how to affix a larger guide for you. As for fishing during slush-like conditions, finesse is not a word I would use to describe one's approach.

Connecting with fish throughout mild winter periods presents some unique challenges. The first thing fish want to do once hooked is head underneath the nearest chunk of shelf ice. Since anglers may only have a few feet of open water to send a drift through, this often means having to perform some fancy rod maneuvering to keep from snapping off. More often than not most of the battle seems to take place with the angler's rod more in the water than out, which can make for some pretty interesting fishing. Anglers fishing atop thick shelf ice should consider bringing a net to help them land fish during those difficult situations where there is nowhere to land a fish. Remember, there are some brute-sized steelhead around at this time and trying to land one alone atop a steep gradient or slippery ice shelf may be next to impossible. Bring a net to avoid disappointment.

❖ Steelhead Through the Ice ❖

During cold Great Lakes winters, the kind that are more characteristic of the region, some diehard steelheaders have managed to cure their cabin fever by pursuing steelhead despite the canopy of ice that has now blocked their river access. These anglers have learned to extend their steelhead season by trading in their long limber noodle rods and neoprene waders in favor of a short, stout piece of graphite and sharp bladed ice augers.

Fishing for steelhead through the ice does require a fair bit of foresight especially for those

In most winter situations steelhead remain steadfast in their position, not moving far for a bait. Trying to pinpoint a fishes exact location may mean drilling a plethora of holes. You will have to work for your fish.

who have yet to forego the adventure. First and foremost, beyond anything else, your safety needs to take precedence when you are dealing with all-ice fishing situations.

Generally speaking, river ice is suitable for fishing once it has acquired a thickness of 4-5 inches (10-12cm). However, it should be understood that I am speaking of the very slow flowing water/marsh areas of lower river regions and that the 4-5 inch (10-12cm) thickness is just a relative guide. Always, always, always check with your local natural resource center or bait and tackle shop as well as friends in order to ensure that ice fishing on the rivers will be safe.

Even with firsthand information it should also be noted that it is the responsibility of each angler to properly assess ice conditions once he arrives.

I always wear a life jacket and carry ice spikes for first ice scenarios and I test the ice for thickness with an ice spud every couple of feet to ensure my safety. I encourage all of you to do the same.

Anglers new to steelheading over river ice should also be aware that first ice is still building and will often boom, crack, snap, and expand while you are fishing. This can often lead to some pretty intense adrenaline overdoses and can make for some anxious moments, however, cracking ice usually is a good indication of new ice forming and that your well-being is not in jeopardy.

Watch for black, blue or clear ice, as it is often the safest ice, and keep an eye out for white or gray areas as they may suggest areas of soft ice. Quite often snow will melt and re-freeze on top of the ice which can also give it a gray or whitish appearance, but if the ice is thick, this should pose no problem for the angler.

Unlike fishing during open-water periods, fishing for steelhead through the ice presents its own unique set of challenges as the open water playing field has now been reduced to the diameter of your auger blades multiplied by the amount of holes you can drill during a day's outing.

Perhaps the greatest challenge for the ice steelheader is simply trying to locate steelhead as they can be widely scattered throughout the entire river

If fish are under your hole expect them to hit almost immediately. After 6 minutes with no hits search new drilling prospects close by as fish may be situated only yards away.

56 | STEELHEAD FLOAT FISHING

system. Since each river system presents us with a different set of circumstances, the only sure way to locate and connect with mid-winter fish is through trial and error and by putting in some good old-fashioned legwork. Of course you can always follow the rest of the crowd but that's taking the easy way out, and besides, scouting new territory often pays larger dividends and will make you a more informed steelheader.

Start looking for fish in the same deep, slow-flowing bend pools, deep runs, and in the deep, slow-flowing estuary water where fish were just prior to freeze up. Also watch for fish to be in the shallows on occasions as well. Keep in mind that unlike the late autumn/early winter period that had most of the fish tightly grouped within the center of deep pools, mid-winter fish will often spread out as they acclimate to colder temperatures.

Effective baits for first ice situations quite often parallel those of the late autumn period, although some special considerations must now be taken into account.

Since first ice is generally four to five inches thick, this often creates ideal conditions to try and tempt holdover fish with searching types of lures such as the Kwikfish.

To fish Kwikfish through the first ice, get on your hands and knees and simply stick the rod down the ice hole and let what little current that may exist transport the lure downstream as you feed out line with an open reel bail. If lure and line stops short of your expectations, close bail and reel in a bit, start the wobbling action, then open the bail again and let the resistance take the lure as you feed out more line.

Forget about using split shot with this method as the currents may be far too light.

Connecting with fish using this method is a real thrill, especially if you are on top of clear, black first ice as you can literally watch the fish twist and fight all around your feet as you work it towards the hole.

Since steelhead may be spread over a wide area within the same piece of holding water, pinpointing their exact location will mean drilling a plethora of holes to try and locate their precise whereabouts. This can quickly turn a day of fishing into a labor intensive endeavor when thick ice conditions prevail, but hey, no one said that ice fishing for steelhead was gonna be easy, in fact steelheaders choosing to pursue their quarry throughout the cold winter period often have their work cut out for them as fish movement during harsh cold mid-winter periods can be extremely limited. This essentially means that you have to go to the fish instead of them coming to you.

To give you an example of the steadfast positioning that fish often take during cold water periods, there have been many instances where I have only caught one fish in a hole only to drill another five or ten feet away to connect with another and so on. These are definitely dormant fish interested in feeding, but not moving.

Another key to locating fish within a holding area is to erase the mindset that fish have to situate over the top of deep water. It seems that once fish have acclimated to the winter water temperatures, they can situate just about anywhere that affords them slack water. This often includes the shallow water margins of pool areas adjacent to deep water.

I have often mistakenly drilled a hole on top of water as shallow as two feet thinking I just wasted my time only to be rewarded with fish. In any event, the key to catching steelhead during the hard water period is to be right over them with the right bait.

Once you have located on top of fish, catching them is mere child's play as they often exhibit eager feeding behaviors despite their lowered metabolisms.

Generally speaking, fish that have been left undisturbed and have received little or no angling pressure will take full advantage of feeding opportunities and will in most cases, hit a bait almost instantaneously. Watch for fish to hit within the first few seconds after dropping your bait down, especially if no one else has attempted to fish the area.

After a minute or two with no hits, start looking to drill holes nearby. After six or seven minutes your chances of connecting with a fish drops considerably as fish simply may not be present.

Some feel this may be a hasty approach but my experience has taught me that fish quickly embrace any feeding opportunities if they are present and that waiting for fish to come to you is a rather unproductive endeavor.

Drilling upwards of five to ten holes per holding area is often your quickest way to success. It can be exhausting work, at times, but productive nonetheless.

Since most Great Lakes regions allow for the use of two rods when ice fishing (check local regulations) leave one in a rod stand while keeping a vigilant watch over it as you drill your subsequent holes.

It is also a great idea to leave your bail open on this reel. Otherwise, a scrappy steelhead may bolt with your rig in tow. Believe me, a rod weaving from side to side along the ice towards the hole makes for a great cardio workout as I have made the mad dash on occasion but have since learned to simply leave the bail open when tending to other holes or a second line.

Contrary to what seems logical to you or I, the drilling of multiple holes, and overhead noises such as walking, or in some cases running, does not seem to scare fish from their holding lies. Fish residing in shallow two foot (.6m) depths also seem unaffected as I have taken them within seconds of drilling a hole right over them. Perhaps they have grown accustomed to such noises as river ice is forever expanding and cracking.

As for bait choices while fishing over the hard top, you have a few options. As already noted, Kwikfish make for great first ice presentation but increasing ice thickness throughout the season may limit their use.

Fish for unmolested steelhead just off the bottom with egg sinkers and floating roe sacs because they are often the most reliable bait. Try pink, chartreuse, white, and orange with contrasting Styrofoam floaters because these will keep baits within a foot off bottom. If you set the hook to quickly and miss a fish while using roe do not despair as fish are more than likely to come back for the missed morsel provided they haven't felt the hook. Remember if fish refuse your roe offerings do not leave the hole without also having tried a black jig as steelies may be targeting stoneflies or dragonfly nymphs. I have had fish refuse my roe offerings on more than one occasion only to have them hit a jig within a minute of sending it down the hole. Lift jigs up and down ever so slightly as this is sure to get a steelhead's attention.

To fight fish through the ice, do so in the traditional sense as a newly augured hole is generally free of sharp ice edges. Don't worry about your line as it rarely brakes despite the punishment that it appears to be taking. Catching a glimpse of your fish as it passes by and watching the water bob up and down in the hole as the fish inches closer can really get the adrenaline pumping. However, fish are often lost when excitement replaces your better judgment. To avoid disappointment and lost fish, refrain from lifting the fish into the hole by grabbing the line. Instead, use the shock absorbing qualities of your short rod, otherwise you risk snapping low stretch fluorocarbon leaders. Getting fish up and out of the hole can be a clumsy task but for the most part simply slide a finger into its gill plate (not gills) and slide the fish onto the ice. Never use a gaff unless you plan on keeping fish.

On cold days keep in mind that prolonged exposure to the elements may begin to freeze the fishes eyes, so release fish quickly.

Since venturing out on the ice often involves the use of several pieces of equipment, you may want to invest in a cheap toboggan to transport all of your ice fishing gear. Drill holes around the parameter for a tow rope (doubles as a lifeline) and for bungee cords to keep your gear in place while en-route. Along with the rest of your ice gear, you may also want to bring extra augur blades as they have a tendency of dulling up after a day or two of hard fishing. Keep them in a hard plastic hinged soap dish along with extra blade bolts and an allen key. Use caution when replacing blades at home or in the field as they are extremely sharp and the last thing you need is an unfortunate accident out in the field.

If the truth be known, ice fishing for steelhead can be the toughest steelhead fishing you will ever encounter as each fish has to be sought out and earned.

For those a little timid about the wintry weather, choose your days; and only venture out when air temps are around the freezing mark. Nobody said you had to be cold to go ice fishing.

➔ Late Winter, Early Spring ✦

With the turning of yet another calendar page to March, anglers begin the countdown towards more favorable spring-like weather that will soon free all rivers and streams of their icy wintry grips.

Ice out conditions though, are largely dependent upon the severity of the winter that prevailed and the developing weather of spring. Generally speaking, river ice and snowpack will either slowly melt and open the rivers, thus providing stable angling conditions, or they will bust wide open with spring rain and rise onto flood plains shutting down the fishing for days to weeks on end.

Although ice out conditions and warmer spring temperatures generally occur by mid to late March the clashing of the seasons can often throw us right back in the cold grips of old man winter.

Late winter storms can take both the steelhead and steelheader by surprise as anglers can be enjoying periods of early spring sunshine one minute only to be violently replaced by cold March winds and heavy lake affect snow the next.

To be quite honest, I absolutely adore these outrageous and wild late season weather scenarios. In fact, some of my best fishing has come during the worst possible blowing, blinding snowstorms. The same kind which seem to obscure your float despite it being straight out in front of you.

For some reason, feeding behavior seems to peek during these turbulent storm-like situations. One such storm presented itself during late March of 2002 while I was fishing in the open water harbor area of Lake Ontario's infamous Ganaraska River. Ironically that same spring storm saw more accumulation of snow then did the entire mild winter.

Drifting in-between the slush that was now forming due to the heavy snow, I connected with steelhead after steelhead all on black number six steelhead jigs. For some reason the fish seemed to be revved by the bad weather. The strong blowing winds had also kicked up some decent wave activity within the harbor which helped to impart realistic movement to the jig which no doubt helped me to connect with these plump-sized early spring steelhead. Whether or not these fish were fresh arrivals or moving back down to the lake in lieu of the deplorable weather conditions is debatable as Great Lakes steelhead are notorious for their back and forth pilgrimages between the lakes and rivermouths as anticipation of the upcoming run grows.

Since the transition from late winter to early spring is often a gradual process, steelhead frequently trickle into the tributaries during opportunistic periods in-between favorable and inclement weather. However, the return of unstable temperatures, sudden weather changes or fluctuating water levels can often impact their upstream progression. It is often during these harsh weather disturbances that steelhead frequently become trapped between wanting to migrate due to their increasing sexual maturity and not being able to do so due to conflicting environmental conditions. These run interruptions often cause steelhead to alter their migration behaviors and enter into a pattern more conducive to holding.

Steelhead that may have already started their upstream runs, may now be forced to abort their early migrations and seek refuge throughout the still and slack water areas discussed earlier in this section. Remember, do no neglect to fish the slow and reversing flows of pool back eddies at this time as they can be steelhead magnets during ill timed drops in temperatures following stable migration types of weather.

As for bait choices for your March presentations, roe wrapped in fluorescent to baby pink shades once again seems to be the predominate color for egg presentations though absolutely, under no circumstances, should you neglect to try black steelhead jigs as March is prime emergence time for the larger early black stoneflies.

If fish have entered a holding pattern due to low water levels they may become stale as angling pressure can turn them off the bite. This is the time to try and provoke a territorial strike out of the larger males. Try tossing K-5 through K-8 Kwikfish. You may also want to try fluorescent orange five-inch jointed benos if you are fishing throughout harbor areas as they often induce strikes even in clear water situations from aggressive territorial pre-spawn males.

Conflicting weather scenario's can quickly send early migrating fish back into a holding pattern. This colossal late winter giant was caught during an early spring snowstorm that more than likely stalled its migration.

Chapter 7
Spring Steelhead

➤ Pre-spawn Water and Migration ←

Generally speaking, fair numbers of pre-spawn spring steelhead begin to trickle in with the ice and slush flows of late winter. Greater numbers of steelhead, however, seem to push upstream during spring run-off or after the floodwaters subside proceeding the ice out period of March and April.

The increased flows and reduced visibility during this time will also release holdover autumn fish from their upstream holding lies and give them the extra push they need to access the upper spawning gravel.

Interestingly enough these migrations are taking place during the same low 32-34°F (0-2°C) water temperatures which earlier had these fish seeking out pool depths throughout the autumn and winter periods.

Perhaps both spring and autumn steelhead have acclimated to the low temperatures throughout the winter and are now being drawn upstream by prolonged photo periods, increased flows, and sexually maturing gonads.

While fishing for pre-spawning migrants, watch for patterns in their migration to emerge. Fish on the move during increased flows and turbidity show little interest in pool depths as their primary focus has now turned to migration. Instead, look for fish to travel close to shore throughout slow-flowing runs as well as slack water or seam area's. Do not be surprised to find fish in shallow one to three feet (.3-.9m) runs close to shore as these are often prime holding areas out from the main flow. On larger rivers, fish may be close to shore throughout seam sections. While in migration mode, steelhead will undoubtedly alternate between holding and moving as they rest in between their migrations. Remember, it is the holding or resting fish that

Fish holding during migration are the most vulnerable to drifted baits. This holding pre-spawn female was caught by Dave Lawson using roe presentation.

Watch for pre-spawn steelhead to selectively feed on the shoreward migrations of the early black stonefly. Once steelhead lock onto these abundant one-inch stoneflies they may totally ignore even the freshest roe presentations. This is the time to make the switch from roe to black jigs. Early black stones emerge form mid-March to April and can easily be seen crawling along snowy stream stretches.

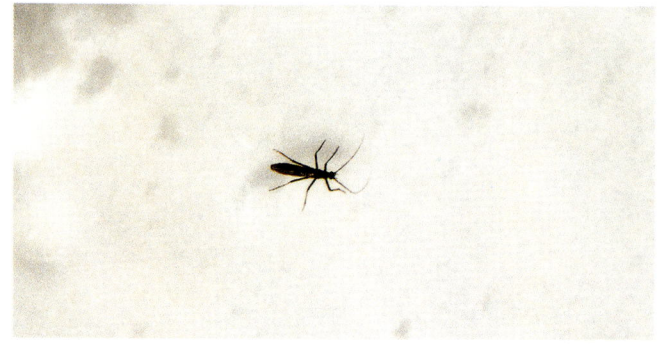

seems the most vulnerable to our presentations. They also seem to hit the first bait that comes their way. More often than not most turbid water holding areas close to shore will only harbor limited fish as they may be spread out, therefore, you may want to take the run and gun approach.

Picking up on this behavior early can mean fishing a lot of holding water rather quickly which may prove beneficial as other anglers are still trying to decipher where the fish are or what they are doing. Work these small, turbid holding areas quickly but be thorough and intuitive enough to surmise when is the best time to relocate to the next piece of holding water.

When visibility in the four- to seven-inch (10-18cm) range, try the larger roe and attractor patterns that we've discussed earlier in the autumn chapter. If conditions are dropping and clearing after ice out fish may be in peak migration mode, only resting for brief periods. These will be the most difficult fish to catch since they are moving more than resting.

Prime water conditions often prevail once visibility increases to between 8-15 inches (20-38cm). The clearing water and pea-green coloration that the rivers take on often make for some of the best float-fishing situations. Roe wrapped in pink, chartreuse, or white are often great bait choices during these clearing conditions, although anglers should not neglect productive plastic alternatives such as ordinary pink gooey bobs, three to four inch (8-10cm) pink plastic worms and 1 1/2 inch (4cm) pearl white or pink plastic tube jigs. Of course black marabou jigs should be added to this list as the early black stoneflies continue to emerge throughout March and April.

As the system continues to drop and clear, watch for fish to gravitate towards deeper runs and pools. Here they will rest throughout the day and attempt to resume their migrations throughout late afternoon periods. Attentive anglers may even observe these late afternoon fish as they can often be seen milling around the heads of pools and venturing into the adjoining shallow flats. Some of these eager fish continue upstream while others make the attempt, but drop back to the pool, opting to run under the cover of darkness.

It should also be noted that while spring migrations of steelhead are progressively working their way upstream, steelhead from the autumn race who made the journey months beforehand are now busy tearing up the gravel, and in most cases, will complete their reproductive duties prior to the arrival of the first spring migrants. These autumn fish seem to spawn in slightly colder water temperatures then their spring spawning cousins as I have documented females digging redds in temperatures as low as 33°F (.5°C).

There is no doubt that aquatic nymphs of several species become dislodged during redd construction and become easy prey item for both yearling and adult steelhead. No wonder our bead-head jig and nymph presentations work so well.

During dry spring situations which offer little in the way of rain or runoff, steelhead may also start their upstream migrations under moderate flow conditions. In this scenario, individuals and loose groups will work their way upstream during the overnight and early morning periods. These nighttime, pre-dawn movements often give their presence away as their large wakes are easily recognizable on mid-sized tributaries. Anglers can often intercept these fish as they seek out temporary holding areas within pools and runs throughout the day.

First-light anglers should focus on the head and midsections of pools and runs but should not neglect to fish the tailouts as some fish may drift slowly backwards as they rest throughout the day. Also watch for migration attempts by these fish to resume during late afternoon.

Flow characteristics of each tributary also seem to dictate the upstream progression of spring runs. Rivers that contain dams with fishways along their water courses, in many cases, seem to stall the upstream passage of fish. Such is the case along Ontario's Ganeraska River. Fish seem to arrive early below the large dam but cannot access the fish ladder until favorable water temperatures raise to at least 41°F (+5°C).

The increased water temperature sparks life into these fish and encourages them to negotiate fishways. However, this happens weeks after they have arrived at the base of the dam. This of course sets back their natural run timing. Rivers and streams with low overhead lamprey barriers can also hold back or stall upstream migrations during years of low spring runoff. Whereas rivers that are free of dams and barriers provide fish with prompt easy upstream and downstream access.

Knowing these flow characteristics is of paramount importance since spawning in some rivers will have already taken place, while in others, it still has yet to occur. Paying attention to such details will help you keep on top of the variable run timings and spawning durations of fish in your region.

➔ Post-spawn Steelhead ←

Steelhead entering tributaries to spawn throughout the spring period often make short-order of the deed and begin dropping out of the system with relative speed. The time it generally takes spring fish to migrate and spawn varies from one region to the next, but the time frame ranges between 2 to 11 weeks (with some exceptions) with the average being approximately 3 to 7 weeks for most Great

Lakes tributaries (D.P. Dodge, R.L. Hassinger, T.M. Stauffer, 1980).

Obviously the autumn migrants take much longer having migrated the previous year. The autumn migrants however, seem to be among the first to spawn over the spring populations and begin dropping out of the system while the spring race is still en route to the spawning gravel (personal observation).

As noted in our last section, rivers that are free of any migration barriers often see the quickest runs as there is nothing to stall or impede the fish. It is in these types of river systems that post-spawn fish begin to show up first, especially if conditions are conducive for early spawning. Watch for drop backs to show up as early as late March to mid-April in lower Great Lakes regions. Some will be from the autumn race, while others may be from the late-winter, early-spring migrations.

Having completed their reproductive duties, steelhead soon revert back to their chrome coloration and reveal the hardship of the spawn through both their physiology and their post-spawn behaviors.

In river systems without migration barriers such as dams, steelhead can migrate, spawn and begin returning to the lake before the regular season opens. Jim Berrard's early season drop back catch was taken in a river section with an all year open season.

Females become but a shadow of their former full-figured forms with their sunken body cavities and half-worn tails, while males exhibit raw undersides and visible scars of supremacy.

Both sexes, however, are said to lose approximately one third of their pre-spawn body weight to the spawn.

Soon after the spawn, steelhead seem to enter a sulking or recuperation phase and can easily be seen situated just under the surface of pools with their heads down and tails up. In upper headwater areas, where fast water prevails over pools, fish will opt to situate in the dead water space along riverbanks. In either situation, these post-spawn behaviors are suggestive of overly exhausted fish in desperate need of rest and recuperation.

While I would not advocate fishing for steelhead that are easily visible and exposed at your feet, fish residing in pools, on the other hand, are a fair challenge albeit they often ignore all presentations. Fortunately, the duration of their recuperation phase is generally brief. It usually lasts a few days to a week. Watch for fish to resort back to opportunistic feeding soon after.

Since not all fish spawn during the exact same time frames they will inevitably be in various stages once they enter the post-spawn phase. Some fish within the same pool will have just entered the post-spawn recuperating phase while their predecessors have already made the transition.

Post spawn steelhead usually situate with their heads down and tails up. This typical behavior may signify overly exhausted fish in need of rest and recuperation. Often these sulking fish are off the bite and not co-operative. Fortunately, this behavior is brief.

Generally speaking, by opening day of trout season most fish will have already recuperated and are easily taken with roe presentations.

Watch for post-spawn steelhead to once again suspend off river bottoms in slower water sections of pools, deep flats, around boulders, and blowdowns, once spring water temperatures begin to increase.

Generally, post-spawn fish will start to suspend in water temperatures around 37-41°F (3-5°C), however, some may sit deeper throughout the water column during up and down fluctuations in water temperatures.

As temperatures start to steadily climb throughout spring most fish will suspend within one to three (.3-.9m) under the surface within these calm water stretches. Expect fish to situate closer to the bottom in faster flowing areas such as runs, troughs, and pockets with riffles.

The fighting capabilities of these post-spawn fish also intensifies with a rise in water temperatures. In fact, their long runs and skyrocketing leaps often leave you wondering whether or not your hooked fish is a fresh migrant.

❖ Angling Pressure ❖

Fishing for steelhead during the first few days after the regular open season can be mere child's play for the novice and experienced alike. However, this soon changes as popular overused presentations are soon rejected by fish that have grown wary of repeated offerings.

Since heavy angling pressure is sure to shut these post-spawn fish down, the steelheader now needs to re-think his post-pressure strategies and bait choices.

Moving off the beaten path to less popular upstream locations is a sure bet for continuous action. Knowing the river system well beforehand, and where fish tend to locate, is a key strategy. Often overlooked, lower river estuaries are also key holding areas that become neglected once the regular trout season is underway. Post-spawn steelhead often congregate here, sometimes in very close proximity to the lake as they wait for increases in lake temperature prior to reentry. Watch for new drop backs to locate throughout these areas as they move downstream during quiet overnight periods.

Anglers choosing to stick to the more popular areas may be fishing for stubborn overly-pressured steelhead. While your chances of hooking these fish may be diminished, all may not be lost as fish will oftentimes hit new baits that have yet to be presented. Avoid roe presentations as it has been way overused and becomes less effective. Even first light roe offerings may be rejected.

Rather, try natural worm presentations such as small enticing red wigglers or trout worms. Impaling several wax worms on a small hook can also prove extremely effective. My first introduction to the effectiveness of wax worms years ago was a humbling experience. I had fished above several spooked fish all afternoon with no hits only to have a passing angler catch a fish on his first drift as he worked his way downstream using these tiny but deadly worms. Needless to say, it was a hard lesson learned.

Other natural clear-water alternatives include live stoneflies that you can easily obtain from underneath nearby boulders. Also search for them in submerged woody debris within log jams or by pealing off the rotten bark of submerged wood.

Although not a familiar bait in Ontario, *Hexagenia* (burrowing mayfly) nymphs are extremely popular south of the border and are sold in many tackle shops. *Hexagenia* nymphs are found throughout most Great Lakes tributaries but have not caught on as much in Ontario as in the United

Nothing shuts fish down faster than heavy angling pressure. Seasoned anglers like George Anderson learned long ago the best fishing is often miles away from the crowds.

States. If you are eager to try them in Ontario, you will have to harvest your own. Look for them throughout the silty, slow-water marsh areas of lower tributaries.

Although delicate, natural single salmon eggs also take their fair share of post-spawn steelhead. Try tying them individually in roe netting to prevent them from tearing off during the cast.

As for your artificial options, lean towards smaller sized baits especially as temperatures and angling pressure increase. Give one-inch tube jigs a try in natural tones such as pearl white, root beer, clear smoke, red/pearl and blue as well as others. Of course marabou are also lethal, in fact, I rely heavily on them for most of my pre- and post-spawn fishing.

My favorite clear-water spring jig color is light olive coupled with grizzly hackle. I developed this color combo after having observed the behavioral drift of sow bugs (crustacean) that took place on the lower tributaries I frequent. These 1/2 inch (1cm) olive crustaceans leave the silty stream bottoms in April and suspend while riding the slow drift. Actively kicking their numerous legs throughout the drift, they are sure to attract attention from suspended steelhead.

Whether or not this jig pattern is suggestive of these migrating crustaceans, or that of small emerging Chinook salmon fry, is debatable. In any event they sure produce when other baits tend to fail. Try number six jigs for best results.

Clear water is also the time to try a variety of nymph patterns. Black, brown, olive or white seem to be the most favored as they best represent the color spectrum of the aquatic community. Try either black or brown nymphs throughout the month of May. Large number 2 to 4 black stonefly nymph patterns will be a great counterfeit of the large stonefly (Pteronarcys dorsata) which are now hatching. Also, try smaller number 12 to 16 brown nymphs as they are suggestive of the Hendrickson mayfly hatch which is also in progress.

Whether you tie your own nymphs or purchase them from your local tackle shops, try using bead-head nymphs as they tend to sink quickly reducing the need for shot closer to the nymph.

Tiny plastic cream colored grubs threaded onto small 1/32 ounce jig heads are also good clear water alternatives. Remember to impart the occasional twitch while using bead-head jigs and nymphs to give the impression of realism to the bait. This will often drive fish over the edge and provoke instinctive strikes.

As water temperatures climb above the 41°F (5°C) mark, do not expect to catch many steelhead on wobbling types of lures. For some unknown reason most steelhead regain their flight responses during increased temperatures and will now become frightened of the lure. Of course, there are always those fish that prove this theory otherwise, however, my experience suggests that it is best to stick with suspended baits under a float.

During stable weather scenarios in the weeks proceeding the season opener, be on the lookout for groups of steelhead to suddenly drop into the pools throughout the day from upstream locations. Also, watch for fish to take up residence in shallow pockets within broken water riffle areas. Fish may tend to emigrate during broad daylight under clear water conditions because of increases in water temperature or extensive fishing pressure from upstream anglers. Oftentimes fish may simply head downstream just because it's time to leave.

In low, clear pressured water scenarios, try the baits suggested above as they are time proven presentations and rarely will you leave the river without having tasted sweet steelhead success.

✦ Rain, Movement, ✦ Locations, and Bait

Just as pre-spawn steelhead are reliant on increases in flow for their upstream migrations, so too are they dependent upon flow increases for their downstream dispersals.

During moderate freshets, post-spawn steelhead move downstream with relative ease and speed, therefore, anglers should eliminate upper fishing areas and re-focus on mid- to lower-river regions. As water starts to drop and clear, try fishing the tailout sections of pools first, as fish will often situate here prior to moving out and into the next set of riffles. Also try seam sections adjacent to fast water as well as around any obstruction such as boulders or blowdowns which break up the flow. You may also want to watch for fish to locate

Pink worms work well in clear and turbid water. Try them in pools for suspended clear water steelhead. Also try them in tailouts as post spawn fish rest before heading downstream during turbid flows.

throughout shallow flowing flats. Since fish have their guard down within turbid flows, roe may produce favorably once again. Try chartreuse, white, or pale yellow. Why fish seem to find renewed interest in this bait after having rejected it during heavily pressured, clear water angling situations often makes me wonder. However, when it comes to steelhead fishing we often find we have more questions than answers. It goes without saying that post-spawn steelhead will also target large dew worm presentations as they are often washed from streambanks during rain events. A great natural worm alternative is a large number two brown steelhead jig. Its large brown profile is often mistaken for a natural worm washed into the drift. Large #2 or #4 black jigs are also productive turbid water presentations. Their silhouettes stand out remarkably within the stained flow. Three- to four-inch plastic worms, whether they be various shades of pink or just plain white, brown or chartreuse, are also popular post-spawn baits during stained spring flows

Don't forget pearl white or glow in the dark tube jigs in your turbid water arsenal as they show up remarkably throughout stained post-spawn flows. Bump up to 1 1/2 to 2 inch (3.9-5cm) sizes for dirty water use. It is interesting to note that as the majority of post-spawn fish are progressively working their way downstream there is a minute segment of the population that is only now starting their upstream spawning migration. Their later run timing may be nature's way of spreading out the hatch times should the emerging crop succumb to untimely flooding or silting. These later spawning fish therefore may be the saving grace of the entire run if such catastrophic floods were to unfold as they occasionally do.

❖ Increasing Temperatures ❖ and Late-season Fishing

Increases in water temperatures during mid- to late-spring periods often begin to take a toll on late departing steelhead. It seems that once water temps have increased to 61°F (16°C) and 20° C adult steelhead often become taxed due to decreasing oxygen levels. At this point, fish frequently go off the feed and become rather lethargic in their behavior. While trying to squeeze out the remaining days of a waning steelhead season anglers should exercise a logistical approach with the best interest of these fish in mind.

Refrain from using overly light two and four pound (.9-1.8kg) fluorocarbon leaders as this will inevitably equate to longer battling times and increased morality. Since fluorocarbon is such a great clear-water tool, I never go lighter than 5.6 pound (2.5kg) test for all my clear water presentations. This hasn't hampered my success rate at all.

Upon quickly landing late season fish, avoid taking them out of the water to remove hooks. I often go barbless for quick release. The less you handle fish this time of year the better. If you desire a quick picture make sure to keep the fish in the water until your fishing partner gets the camera ready.

Remember, you are responsible for your fish. Take the time to resuscitate tired fish until they show signs of recovery. If using proper equipment and release techniques this shouldn't take more than a few seconds.

While there are some that would not advocate fishing for steelhead during increased water temperatures, I feel that if done properly the resource is no worse for the wear.

I often make subsequent trips to slow pool areas where I have caught and released fair numbers of fish during the late season and have found no signs of mortality. Fighting fish fast with appropriate terminal tackle seems to be the key this time of year.

❖ Post-spawn Movements ❖ and Lake Dispersal

What happens once our post-spawn spring steelhead re-enter their large lake feeding environment. According to a 1981/82 study—completed by James M. Haynes, David C. Nettles, Kevin M. Parnell (Department of Biological Sciences), Michael P. Voiland (New York Sea Grant Extension) Robert A. Olson, and Jimmy D. Winter (Environmental Resources Center Sunny College at Fredonia)—entitled "Movements of Rainbow Steelhead Trout in Lake Ontario," the majority of radio tagged and temperature-sensing post-spawn steelhead in a Lake Ontario test creek exhibited east-west near shore movements. Reversals in direction were also common and are said to be associated with near shore currents and wind. The duration of these near shore movements was brief, lasting sometimes only a few days to a few weeks from April to July.

This depends on the spring weather. During cooler springs near shore thermal bars take longer to form, often concentrating fish close to shore. During warmer years, thermal bars form and move offshore more quickly and fish disperse more rapidly. Offshore movements of post-spawn steelhead often coincide with increases of near shore surface temperatures warming above 50°F (10°C) in spring. Offshore anglers are also included in the study and report some of the best catches in May, after the near shore temperatures exceeded 50°F (10°C) were taken more than 1.9 miles (3km) offshore and were very near the lake surface under slicks of insects and debris concentrated at the surface by thermal fronts.

Chapter 8
Involvement and the Future

As the wild steelhead fishery continues to decline throughout the lower Great Lakes regions there seems to be a lot of discussion on how we can best curb the downward trend and help restore the steelhead fishery back to its once flourishing state.

Some argue that steelhead limits are too liberal and the subsequent exploitation of the fishery by increased numbers of anglers each season is quickly leading to the downfall of the fishery. While this is a valid argument, the science behind the fishery suggest that it would take more than just a meager fish reduction to offset the downward spiral. Some would suggest that supplemental stocking of hordes of cookie cutter hatchery fish will quickly solve this problem, but again, fishery science has proven otherwise. There are countless fishery studies on the topic of hatchery fish being stocked on top of wild populations and I have yet to come across one which suggests that it is a productive practice.

For the most part, hatchery fish have been raised in a controlled environment with controlled feeding regimes. With such luxuries they become conditioned and lose their flight responses since they are not exposed to predators. Once released into the wild they often prey on smaller yearling steelhead, contributing to further wild steelhead losses. With poor flight responses they become susceptible to predation from birds and mammals. The long and short of it is that they are poor products

Concerned about the state of your local steelhead fishery? Then why not lend a hand to the numerous steelhead organizations that partake in stream rehabilitation projects each summer. Stabilizing streambanks and tree planting provide both adult and emerging steelhead with a healthier habitat. Here, the Nottawasaga Steelheaders "put a little back."

when compared to their wild cohorts. Generally speaking hatchery fish have a return rate of .5 to 3% whereas fish born to the wild assume a 5 to 10% survival rate. There is no denying that nature does a much better and efficient job at seeding the population. So we are back to square one in terms of our declining fishery. All is not lost, however, as there is plenty that we as individuals can do to help offset our declining steelhead numbers. Not to sound redundant but you can start by releasing most if not all of your catch of wild steelhead. Anglers wishing to keep the odd fish for roe and consumption should consider that the size of a kept fish can make a difference throughout the population. Generally speaking steelhead biologists have concluded that steelhead between 20-26 inches (66cm) are maiden spawners and are therefore spawning for the first time. These fish should be released to give them a chance to contribute to the overall population.

According to a report compiled on the Brule River in Wisconsin, the Department of Natural Resources suggests selectively harvesting larger, older fish over 26 inches (66cm) (preferably males). By keeping a larger fish you have insured that all fish have at least spawned once. This ensures that enough eggs are laid and that all have been able to pass their genes back into the population.

Despite what the Wisconsin report suggests, anglers should also consider that the larger repeat spawners also act as important buffers during years which produce weak year classes of offspring. The larger repeats can re-seed a stream on subsequent spawning runs to make up for the poor crop.

As you can see, each spawning fish—maiden or repeat—plays a vital role among the entire population. If you really must keep a fish I would suggest keeping a hatchery fish that is easily distinguished with a fin clip. Besides, their presence is scientifically known to contaminate the wild gene pool. If you must keep a couple of wild fish I would recommend keeping one under and one over 26 inches (66cm) in areas that do not already have a size restriction. This way you help to balance out the loss. Please remember to limit your catch and that it is much cheaper to buy fish at the market for food than it is to fill up the gas tank and catch them yourself. Also remember that roe isn't the end-all bait that will help you catch fish as I have clearly demonstrated throughout this text.

Aside from practicing catch-and-release as well as selective harvest, concerned steelheaders can also become involved in maintaining our wild fish stocks by participating in local stream rehabilitation projects. Each summer, across many Great Lakes regions, concerned members of local steelhead organizations roll up their sleeves and become physically involved in restoring vitally important upstream spawning and nursery habitats. The work is often physical but well worth the rewards. Projects usually range from the removal of river clogging log jams, which block both upstream and downstream migration access, to bank stabilization and tree planting, which helps to prevent bank erosion and provides shading for emerging young. So, you can see there is something that we all can do to help the future of our fabulous steelhead fishery. All that it takes is commitment, a little time, and will. Please get involved in your local stream rehabilitation efforts and in the words of the Nottawasaga Steelheaders "put a little back."

To learn more about stream rehabilitation in the Lake Ontario Region please contact the Nottawasaga Steelheaders at www.nottawasaga.org, as well as the Credit River Anglers Association at www.craa.on.ca.

Chapter 9
Float Reels and How to Cast Them

Throughout the early steelheading era of the 1970s and 80s spinning reels were the reels of choice for many Great Lakes steelheaders. However, things have certainly changed over the last decade or more and today, anglers serious in their pursuit of Great Lakes steelhead, have made the transition from spinning to float reel.

The change from spinning to float reels was a slow and gradual process, yet today, float reels have become so popular throughout some Great Lakes regions that they dominate a lot of the local float fishing scene.

So why are float reels so much more popular today than the standard spinning reel? To start, float reels offer us what spinning reels could not, that being uninterrupted drifts and more precise presentations. Since most float reels spin on a bearing system, anglers can now simply let even modest currents strip line from the reel without having to do it manually.

This is extremely advantageous because it allows for greater line control, especially when trotting a float through slow, moderate, and fast flows. The free spooling drum also allows for precise slack line adjustments, therefore allowing for a taunt line between rod and float. This ultimately equates to quicker hooksets and essentially more fish.

Since float reels have become the ultimate tool for precision float control their popularity has grown exponentially among Great Lakes steelheaders. However, once the newbie angler purchases his first float reel, he is often left to his own resources in terms of learning how to properly cast. Learning to cast from friends that may have some casting

Pinch line ahead of the reel with your forefinger and thumb while the line below this pinch point rests on your remaining fingers.

experience is often a great starting point but, they may have picked up on some bad casting practices which can lead to further casting problems down the line.

The following casting information should provide you with enough instruction to nail down the basics and through practice, eventually help you to achieve distance and accuracy throughout your cast.

➔ Preparing the Cast ←

Preparing for your first cast generally starts in the comfort of your own home. Most novice float reel advocates generally start by overspooling the reel with line. This can easily lead to backlashes and overruns. Generally speaking, fill your spool to within 3/16 to 1/4 inch (5-7mm) of the rim. Use a cheap brand of line for spool backing, then a more reputable manufacturer for your main line. Prior to casting, your body positioning should also be considered since it is a key factor for the beginner to make a successful cast. As you progress, you may alter your standing position. Generally, start by placing your right foot in front of you while transferring your weight to your left leg. Provided that you cast with your right hand, bring your rod up to the twelve o'clock position and let out enough line so that your float is just above your head. This line will assist you to make a pendulum type cast. At this point, the line and float is now in front of you. Next, slightly twist or pivot to the left with the rod held high above your left shoulder. Maintain pressure on the spool with the baby finger of your rod hand to prevent line from spooling off. Using your left hand, pinch the line just forward of the reel with your fore finger and thumb while the line below this pinch point rests on your remaining fingers.

➔ Executing the Cast ←

When you feel comfortable enough to execute a cast, drop the rod down and cast with a forward sweeping pendulum motion (transfer weight to right leg at this point). At the exact same time that you begin this pendulum cast, pull line down and slightly back from the reel. With the reel drum spinning (the pinky finger on your reel hand should be pointing out of the way), and handles tilted slightly upward (this helps prevent backlashes), release the line that you have been pinching with your forefinger and thumb. You now want to use these two fingers to form a circle acting as a guide while the line feeds out. (You may even decide to just use the inside of your thumb for this.)

*Pull line down and back while tilting the reel slightly upwards during the cast.
This helps to prevent line from wrapping around handles and the back of the reel.*

CHAPTER 9: FLOAT REELS AND HOW TO CAST THEM | 69

Using your forefinger and thumb will help prevent backlashes and help keep the line from wrapping around the back of the reel. Should you still experience handle wrap, try tilting the reel slightly so that the handles are facing down midway through the cast. What also needs to be considered during the cast is that the reel must spin equal to the amount of force that is being exerted through the rod, otherwise your entire presentation is likely to boomerang right back towards you.

An alternative casting method which I often use is to raise your rod over and back from your left shoulder. Your reel should now be just above your left shoulder as well. All of your weight should now be transferred to your left leg. (Finger positioning of the line remains the same as the above casting method.) Next, pull the line down from the reel and at the exact same time execute the overhead cast while transferring your weight to your right leg. As you cast the rod forward (overhead) in the direction of the water, follow through with the reel back to the normal forward drifting or hanging position. This is a great distance casting method when streams are crowded and there isn't enough room to execute a pendulum type of side cast, it also works great when friends want to chat while standing on your left hand casting side.

Both of the above casting techniques should be executed with one fluent motion. Also keep in mind that timing within the cast is absolutely crucial. Proper timing will mean all the difference between a well-placed cast and a brain knurling backlash. Once you have mastered the fundamentals of casting, you may tweak the basics to suit your own personal casting preference.

✤ Casting Don'ts ✤

Do not, under any circumstance, cast off the face of the reel. In this scenario, line is feathered off a

Form a partial circle using your forefinger and thumb, this will act as a guide for your line to flow through while your reel is spinning. You may want to hold this hand slightly away from the rod and reel. This technique also prevents line from wrapping around handles and back of reel. Note: Steps 2 and 3 should be done simultaneously.

stationary spool much in the same manner as a spinning reel. Although you will achieve distance with this cast, you will also be rewarded with severe line twist. Before you start cursing the line manufacturers for your casting woes, keep in mind that this is an improper casting technique. If you must cast off the face of the reel then add a barrel swivel above your float to help offset line twist.

✢ Final Word on Casting ✢

If executed properly, the aforementioned casting instructions will never leave you with any sort of line twist. The casting instructions may sound or look a little intimidating at first, but believe me, they are really quite simple. My only other advice is to get out and practice as much as you can. You may even want to practice with larger floats with added weight to help you sort through the inertia and timing of your casts.

Do not attempt distance casting at first because you may only succeed in frustrating yourself which will discourage any further progress. Instead, use the above techniques to gently lob out baits until you have acquired the proper feel for casting. Once you have the basic fundamentals down, casting distance will soon come naturally.

✢ Fighting and Landing Fish ✢

Perhaps the other great benefit of using float reels is that they allow us to fight fish one-on-one without any mechanical intervention. Although some float reel manufacturers include a drag system on their models, most anglers prefer to match wits with an out-of-control steelhead and do battle with the reel in free spool. In this manner it is up to the angler to draw upon his experience and discretion while testing the limits of his terminal tackle. Some say this gives the fish a sporting chance, while others just like the fact that it is a more challenging prospect.

Generally speaking, to fight fish while using a float reel one needs to apply just the proper amount of pressure on the reels rim to tire the fish. Personally, I use the baby finger of my rod hand, however, there are those that prefer to palm the reel with their reeling hand. This, of course, all boils down to personal preference.

Fighting fish without a mechanical drag creates more of a challenge and tests the anglers skill. For some it is a more intriguing way to catch steelhead.

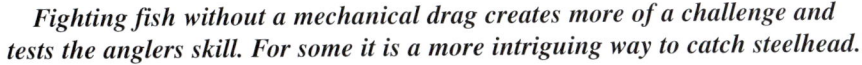

CHAPTER 10
BUILDING BALSA FLOATS

Once steelhead have all but left their spring spawning tributaries and re-entered their large lake feeding grounds, the float fisherman will not get another crack at them until mid to late September.

While some steelheaders opt to chase alternative fish species throughout the summer, others, such as myself, use part of the brief summer period to prepare for these first autumn migrants.

Part of my preparation involves building my own float supply in anticipation of the upcoming season. For steelheaders interested in building their own balsa floats, I can tell you from personal experience that nothing in the world of steelheading is quite more exhilarating than catching a fish on one's own homemade tackle. Not only does it give you a greater sense of accomplishment, but it also adds to the total angling experience.

If the truth be known, building your own homemade balsa floats is a rather simple endeavor. A few common household tools, such as a coping saw, a drill, a 1/16 (2mm) drill bit, hacksaw, a metal file and some sandpaper are all you really need.

The balsa wood you will need is available at most hobby shops. Purchase long 36 inch (91cm) square pieces. To make grayling style floats (inverted tear drop) you will require a square 3/4 x 3/4 piece of balsa 36 inches (1.9 x 1.9 x 9cm) long. For avon styles purchase a square 5/8 x 5/8 piece of balsa 36 inches (1.6 x 1.6 x 9cm) long. Purchase the square strips as they are easier to cut with a coping saw. If you own a band saw then you can purchase blocks of balsa to cut into square lengths. You will also need to purchase a 36 inch (91cm) length of solid metal rod 1/8 inch (3.5mm) in diameter. Purchase them at larger hardware stores. For medium-sized grayling floats measure and cut into one inch lengths (2.5cm). For avons cut into 1 and 11/16 inch lengths or 5 cm. Next insert the 1/16 inch (2mm) drill bit into the drill and drill a hole through the center of each piece of wood. You will now need to cut a 4 3/4 inch (12cm) piece from the metal rod. Once that is done you should file one end down so that it resembles the pointed stem of a float. In this manner it will be far easier to insert the square piece of balsa. Next, take out the drill bit and insert the 4 3/4 inch (12cm) metal rod and tighten. Slide on a piece of the pre-cut/pre-holed balsa. At this point you will notice that the hole diameter of the drilled balsa is smaller than the 1/8 inch (3.5mm) metal rod. That's okay, work the balsa up the metal rod. The hole will expand as you slide it on. Work the square piece of wood up to within an inch or so of the metal rod where it meets the drill chuck. Next, cut up some two inch (5cm) square pieces of 120 to 150 grain sandpaper. Put on a pair of safety glasses to keep balsa dust out of your eyes and nose. Next, hold the drill on a work table facing you and squeeze the handle with your thumb. This will obviously start the chuck, metal rod and balsa

Start the drill spinning then begin to shave and mold the soft balsa with medium 120 - 150 grain sandpaper

After float is shaped smooth it over with a lighter grain of sandpaper.

spinning. When you are ready, take your piece of sandpaper and start shaving the balsa. You may want to move the sandpaper up and down the float to shave off equal amounts. (The beautiful thing about balsa is that it is soft and is easily molded into our float shapes.) Shave the square piece of wood until it is equally round along its side. Next, work the sandpaper over the top of the float until it takes on an oval appearance. This now becomes the top of the float. With this section complete, start to shave the bottom section until it narrows towards the metal rod. Finish the rough float off with some light sandpaper to give it a smooth finish. (You can also use this same method to shave and make the avon style of floats.)

Obviously, your first number of floats will not resemble anything you would want to fish with, but that's okay because balsa wood is very inexpensive.

You more than likely will have to make several practice floats until you get the feel of how to properly shave and mold the balsa. Once you have a few float bodies that you are happy with, then it is time to proceed with the next step. Next, you will need a stem for your float. You can use either a 1/8 inch (3.5mm) wooden dowel (available at hobby shops) or bamboo skews (available at department stores).

You can cut them into preferred sizes to suit your needs. I generally cut mine into 3 3/4 inch (12cm) lengths. Use a pencil sharpener to round off dowel ends and sandpaper for the bamboo skews. Next, assemble balsa and stem to your preference. Staining your floats is optional. Dry with a paper towel. The next step is painting. Stir paint thoroughly and pour into a small plastic cup. (An empty egg carton will also suffice.) Dip float upside down in a white enamel paint—found at hobby stores. You may require two or more coats for best results. (Let the first coat dry before applying the second.) The next step is to let the float dry by sticking them upside-down in a piece of Styrofoam. Once dried, dip in fluorescent orange or chartreuse and let dry. To give the float a durable shiny finish, dip several times in verathane clear finish (clear gloss) available at hardware stores. Let dry before re-dipping.

Once you have the float building basics down and become familiar with the process, you will soon find that each subsequent float you make will look better than the last.

Be forewarned, making your own floats can become addictive. Practice making different shapes and sizes to suit the varying water types you will encounter throughout your travels.

Make floats in various shapes and sizes to suit all your stream fishing needs. These floats are ready for paint and finishing.

CHAPTER 10: BUILDING BALSA FLOATS | 73

CHAPTER 11
CHINOOK SALMON

✧ Historical perspective ✧

When shipping canals were first constructed back in the 1800s and 1900s not only did they open the gateway for easier trade throughout the Great Lakes region but they also created easier access for several evasive exotics, some of which soon brought native Great Lakes fish populations to the edge of extinction.

Perhaps the most prolific and destructive of all the exotics was the parasitic lamprey.

Sea lampreys were responsible for major fishery declines throughout the 1940s and 1950s; in addition, industrial pollution and exploitation were counteracting with Lamprey populations and rendered much of the Great Lake fishery void by 1960. Introduced exotic species such as alewife and smelt were also using shipping canals to access the upper Great Lakes during the late 1800s (alewife) and early 1900s (smelt).

Mid-August is none to soon to start fishing harbor areas. The key is cool temperatures and wet summers.

The loss of predator fish throughout the Great Lakes ecosystem during the lamprey invasions of the 1940s and 50s created a distinct imbalance within the food chain community.

It was also evident at this time that the nutrient levels of the Great Lakes were increasing—the likely byproducts of industry and agriculture. Both non-organic and synthetic fertilizers, phosphate detergents, and human waste collectively led to accelerated algae blooms across the lakes which only enhanced the food production of phytoplankton and zooplankton which are the main dietary components of both the alewife and smelt.

Alewives and smelt that were once preyed upon by indiscriminate lake trout were now left alone in their nutrient rich environments to propagate the four corners of the five Great Lakes. Unimpeded, they overpopulated the ecosystem and during the 1960s they were declared the most abundant fish species throughout the entire Great Lakes watershed.

The overabundance of alewives resulted in a high mortality rate especially during shoreward spawning migration where alewife populations are very susceptible to fluctuating water temperatures. Large-scale public concern grew throughout the 1960s as the general health the lake and its encompassing tributaries was in an advance state of neglect. Realizing that the waterways were in a state of decline, the government soon constructed sewage plants and started regulating population discharges from the industrial sector. As mitigation efforts continued to restore the aquatic integrity to the depleted ecosystem, the US Fish and Wildlife Service searched for ways to eradicate, or control, sea lamprey populations. In 1958 it was discovered that the chemical TFM3 was an effective agent that could destroy lamprey larvae while having a minimal impact on the existing fish and invertebrate community.

With lamprey populations somewhat under control by the mid 1960s and with the reversal of man's deleterious assault on the environment, it was now time to embark on a management plan to restore equilibrium within the lakes.

Alewife and smelt abundance prompted fishery officials from around the Great Lakes to reintroduce the predator component back into the ecosystem. Michigan led the way by planting 850,000 five-inch (12cm) Oregon coho smolts in 1966. Coho found the lakes' abundant forage base very accommodating. The first reported coho catch came some three months later and it had tripled its release length from 5 to 15 inches (12-38cm). By the autumn of 1967, anglers were battling with coho up to 15 pounds (6.9kg). After witnessing the success of the Michigan coho initiative, the remaining Great Lakes soon followed Michigan's lead. Coho plantings took place in Lake Superior in 1966, and in Lake Huron in 1967. Coho plantings also occurred in Lake Ontario in 1968 and Lake Erie in 1967. However, this wasn't the first time the coho was introduced to the lower lakes. Initial plantings for Lake Ontario coho took place in 1919 and Lake Erie in 1933, however, no successful propagation was known to exist as the likely result of an environment under siege.

As the coho salmon initiatives were gaining in angler popularity plans were underway to introduce yet another West Coast contemporary. Soon the Chinook salmon would join its West Coast cousin in the feeding frenzy encompassing the Great Lakes.

Chinooks were introduced into Lake Michigan, Huron, and Superior in 1967 and in Lake Ontario (New York) in 1969, Lake Erie in 1970, and lastly Lake Ontario (Canadian side) in 1971. This would not be the first time Chinook plantings were to take place throughout the Great Lakes. Initial attempts to stock the Great Lakes with Chinooks occurred primarily during 1873, and like the coho, no self-sustaining populations would prevail. Subsequent attempts by Ontario took place from 1919 to 1925, but all attempts were also unsuccessful.

The Chinook initiative finally did take root throughout the late 1960s and 70s and along with its coho cousin it gave birth to a multibillion dollar a year sports fishery.

✥ Chinooks from Shore ✥

Since a Chinook salmon lives most of its life in large, open waters of the Great Lakes, they are generally taken far offshore from boats throughout the summer months. However, once those summer months wane into early autumn those mature Great Lakes feeding machines soon begin the search for their rivermouth stocking sites and rivers of natural origins.

Like their steelhead cousins, it seems that decreasing daylight hours, maturing gonads, and cooler temperatures are the environmental catalysts that start their shoreward migrations.

Once Chinook locate off of rivermouths, they become a sporting challenge for the pier and breakwall bunch who have been eagerly awaiting their arrival. Although early September is generally accepted as being prime time for the pier or breakwall fisherman, many fish will start showing up well beforehand if presented with the proper environmental conditions. Mid August is none too soon to start fishing harbor areas as early-arriving fish are often eager to start their upstream migrations. The key to look for is cooling water temperatures. (The irony about fishing mid August is that the pier angler will often hookup with early catches of harbor sniffing chinnys while the charter boat captains are taking clients far offshore into deep water.) If you do decide to pursue the cruising/staging chinnys of mid August the best times seem to be throughout the quiet overnight hours, or in that hour just before dawn. Staging chinnys will often make overnight and pre-dawn pilgrimages closer to rivermouths while some may even venture into the actual harbor and rest at the first shallow water section. The overnight periods seem to appeal to fish mainly because there is no boat traffic. As for your nighttime lure choices you simply cannot go wrong using glow-in-the-dark casting spoons, fish hit these lures because of their West Coast lineage. Watch for calm lake conditions when opting to cast in the overnight hours as fish seem better able to chase down these glowing presentations.

Jointed body baits such as J-13 Rapala's and a variety of casting spoons such as Little Cleo's and Crocodiles are all productive lure choices for the pier fisherman.

Anglers opting to fish the more sane hours of first light should consider that overnight cruising chinnys will soon start to make their way back to the lake once the sun starts to creep up past the horizon. This is a good time to start working the entire harbor area. This often means doing a lot of fan casting and moving around until you meet up with migrating fish. Your other option is to cast out into the lake from the pier as fish head back out to deep water. Also consider that early season fish do not tend to mill around much after the sun has come up. This means you should consider packing up before 9 in the morning.

Generally speaking, the early mid August pier action can be boom or bust. Perhaps the greatest influence that will determine whether or not fish will be present is the weather. By this I do not mean how the weather was in the last few days, but rather, how it unfolded throughout the entire summer.

Experience has taught me that a summer with prolonged rain seems to attract fish to rivermouths sooner. It is also interesting to note that summers which produce above average rainfall quite often encourage upstream migration of salmon as early as mid to late July, therefore, it really pays to be a weather watcher. During hot, dry summers that produce drought, fish tend to prolong their lake occupancy and can be out of pier-reach until late September or, in adverse cases, October.

During summers with a normal weather regime, watch for greater numbers of Chinook to be resting off rivermouth by early to mid September. If rivers are large, deep and sustain ample flow, then fish migration will occur provided there are suitable water temperatures.

For small to mid-sized rivers some fish will chance the shallow conditions, but most will remain off of rivermouths while they await autumn rains or until overmaturing gonads force them upstream. The preferred lure and bait choices for daytime pier and breakwall anglers are heavy 2/5 to 1/2 ounce casting spoons, jointed body baits, and bottom plunking with roe.

Some of my favorite casting spoons are the Gibbs Rainbow Croc, Luhr Jensen Crocodile and Little Cleos. Try silver spoons with accenting blue, green and orange colors. Hammered spoons also have their days.

My favorite daytime spoon color, believe it or not, is glow-in-the-dark pattern. For reasons unknown to myself, Chinook really love this color.

As for jointed body baits, one can never go wrong with large J-13 Rapalas. In clear water situations Chinook smash J-13 rainbow trout patterns with reckless abandon. I have also had phenomenal success with the chartreuse silver patterns during both clear and stained conditions. If the truth be known, I never go near an autumn pier without a tackle tray full of these productive body baits.

Plunking for salmon with roe, or in some cases marshmallows is a relaxing way to connect with cruising Chinook, however, it should be noted that physical transformations are now changing within the fish. One of which alters the way they breath.

Quite often fish will cruise with their jaws gaping which subsequently leads to your line and bait becoming entangled in their mouths and teeth. In most cases fish hooked in this manner will shake loose and you won't have them on for long. This is not to say that Chinook will not take a suspended bait, only that quite often they swim into it rather than actually eating the offering.

Instead of fishing the bottom, try chucking lures. This way, you know you are outwitting fish instead of them swimming into your bait.

Like steelhead fishing from rivermouths and piers, wind direction means everything in terms of your success, so expect fish to move inshore during periods of onshore winds. Here they will mill around rivermouths all day long especially during overcast conditions. Once moderate onshore winds are accompanied by showers or rain, you may see Chinook swimming along the outside of breakwalls as they search for the actual rivermouth. (Onshore winds most likely disperse river scents all around the mouth and back to shore on either side of the breakwall.) If you arrive to find the wind and wave activity pounding one side of a pier than chances are that cruising and staging fish will relocate to the opposite pier where waters are a fair bit calmer. Here, salmon are out of the heaviest wave activity and can cruise the intermixing choppy and calm water regions looking for baitfish trying to escape from the pounding surf.

Another behavior the pier and breakwall bunch should be on the lookout for is jumping rivermouth fish. Just why salmon begin jumping in and around rivermouth regions still remains a mystery. Some speculate that the large females are trying to loosen or break their skein membranes, however, jumping is also typical for large pre-spawn males.

Watching fish jump all around a pier location can really enthuse and motivate anglers at first. However, once you have tried everything in your tackle box twice, it soon becomes clear that these skyward jumping salmon are off the feed and want little or nothing to do with your jointed plug or spoon presentations.

This typical behavior is often sporadic and can last for several days at a time. Subsequent jumping may also be re-kindled throughout their rivermouth residency, although once fish stop jumping, they seem to regain their aggressive demeanor and will resume normal feeding activity.

⇥ Equipment ⇤

Since Chinook salmon in some regions have the potential of growing to sizes in excess of 30 pounds (13.6kg), I would not recommend you use your valued steelhead equipment as part of your pier fishing arsenal.

Long, limber noodle rods are best used on river steelhead and not on muscle-packed lake bound Chinook. Instead of cracking out the steelhead gear prematurely, why not try using a downrigger rod. A beefy 8 1/2 foot (2.6m) downrigger rod has enough backbone to deliver spoons into the far reaches of the lake with the added benefit of being able to withstand the brutal punishment that a hefty Great Lakes Chinook can dish out.

Rather than burning out the drag on your favorite mid-sized steelhead reel bump up to a larger reel with more guts. For years I have come to rely on an old favorite. It may be an old dinosaur, but my Mitchel 300A reel can turn around any Chinook heading stateside. The large spool capacity also permits for ample yardage of 10-12 pound (4.5-5.4kg) test line. Baitcasters are common reel choices that can also hold large line volumes. Some models seem to cast further than others. So you will need to do your homework in this regard. Also, don't forget the all-important long-handled net.

⇥ Chinook Fishery, Past and Present ⇤

Although the Chinook stocking initiatives continue today, it does so at a reduced capacity when compared to the 1960 efforts. This is due to a number of variables which all link back to the food chain. Once nutrient levels from fertilizers and phosphate detergents were reduced, it set off a chain of events that would soon cause concern with fisheries officials. It seems the reduction in lake-wide nutrients also reduced microscopic plankton (phytoplankton and zooplankton) which were the main dietary component of both the alewife and smelt populations.

By the late 1980s the Lake Michigan alewife population had collapsed, the likely result of three poor successive spawning years, a suppressed food supply, and stress. Chinook survival declined rapidly as the stress of chasing scarce alewives made them vulnerable to deadly viral diseases.

Fishery officials were wary that the same fate would meet the Lake Ontario salmon population. Declining nutrient and plankton production left Ontario baitfish smaller and less abundant through the 1980s. The potential for salmonid populations to exceed the baitfish supply prompted public consultation where it was decided that in order to reduce the risk of an all-out alewife collapse that stocking of all salmonids needed to be reduced to give alewife populations a chance to rebound from their spiraling downward cycle. The decision to reduce stocking by 50% was made in 1991. This reduction allowed baitfish numbers to balance out and by the mid 1990s stocking numbers were moderately increased.

Today, over 160 exotics and counting have established themselves throughout all of the Great Lakes. How they biodiversify, what impact they will have on our bait and sports fishery remains to be seen. Needless to say, trying to maintain equilibrium with the lakes when faced with re-emerging challenges of the past (lampreys) and those about to enter the Great Lakes door (exotics) is a balancing act at even the best of times. Fortunately for us, the ecological balance is still in our favor.

Cool overcast autumn weather can also influence near shore movements. Note the boat in the left of the picture. Fish are often closer than most people think.

BIBLIOGRAPHY

A Report on Nottawasaga River Rainbow Trout. Nottawasaga Steelheaders, Nottawasaga Valley Conservation Authority and Ministry of Natural Resources. 1998.

Biette, R.M., D.P. Dodge, R.L. Hassinger and T.M. Stauffer. *Life History and Timing of Migrations and Spawning Behavior of Rainbow Trout Populations of the Great Lakes.* Canadian Journal of Fisheries Aquatic Sciences, 1981.

Brule River Steelhead: *Understanding Natures Effects*, Wisconsin Department of Natural Resources, 1997.

Burgner, R.L., J.T. Light, L. Margolis, T. Okazaki, A. Tautz and S. Ito. *Distribution and Origins of Steelhead Trout (Oncorhynchus Mykiss) in Offshore Waters of the North Pacific Ocean.* International North Pacific Fisheries Commission. Bulletin Number 51, 1992.

Combs, Trey. *The Steelhead Trout.* Frank Amato Publications, Portland OR, 1988.

Goodyear, C.S., T.A. Edsall, D.M. Ormsby Dempsey, G.D. Moss, and P.E. Polanski. *Atlas of the Spawning and Spawning and Nursery Area's of Great Lakes Fishes.* 14 vols. U.S. Fish and Wildlife Service, Washington, DC., 1982.

Haynes, James, David Nettles, Kevin Parnell, Michael Voil, Robert Olson, and Jimmy D. Winter. *Movement of Rainbow Steelhead Trout in Lake Ontario and a Hypothesis for the Influence of Spring Thermal Structure.* International Association of Great Lakes Research, 1986.

Lake Ontario Fisheries Discussion Papers. Ministry of Natural Resources, 1996.

MacKay., H.H.. *Fishes of Ontario, Rainbow Trout.* Department of Lands and Forests.

Pratt, Dennis, Bill Blust. *The Life Story of a Brule River Steelhead.* 1991.

Rand, Peters, Donald Stewart, Paul Seelbach, Michael Jones, Leslie Wedge. *Modeling Steelhead Population Energetics in Lake Michigan and Ontario.* American Fisheries Society, 1993.

Seelbach, Paul W. *Effect of Winter Severity on Steelhead Smolt Yield in Michigan: An Example of the Importance of Environmental Factors in Determining Smolt Yield.* North American Journal of Fisheries Management, 1987.

Seelbach, Paul W. *Population Biology of Steelhead in a Stable-Flow, Low-Gradient Tributary of Lake Michigan and Ontario.* American Fisheries Society ,1993.

Stauffer, Thomas M., *Age, Growth and Downstream Migration of Juvenile Rainbow Trout in a Lake Michigan Tributary.* American Fisheries Society, 1972.

The Great Lakes, An Environmental Atlas and Resource Book., U.S. Environmental Protection Agency, Great Lakes National Program Office.

Also Available from Frank Amato Publications

SIDE-DRIFTING FOR STEELHEAD
J.D. Richey

There are about as many ways to describe side-drifting as there are anglers practicing it, but one thing's for sure, it's a very effective way to catch steelhead. J.D. Richey is one of the top side-drifting guides on the West Coast, and in this book he shares everything you need to know to become a successful side-drifter. Best described as a family of techniques, side-drifting includes three methods—freedrifting, side gliding, boondogging. Each method has its own chapter where the concepts and tactics are discussed, then a chapter on the basic gear you'll need for that technique. Also included are special tips and tricks from guides and expert anglers, all of whom contributed greatly to the information in this book. You will learn all there is to know about this highly effective, and at times controversial, steelhead method from the best!

SB: $15.95
ISBN: 1-57188-350-9
UPC: 0-81127-00184-2
Available January 2005

SMOKING SALMON & STEELHEAD
Scott & Tiffany Haugen

Among the many benefits of fishing is the chance to bring home the occasional salmon for the smoker. But are you tired of using the same old recipe? If so, the Haugens have done all the experimenting for you. The result is this book, filled with 54 wet and dry brine recipes, including: sweet teriyaki, tropical tang, extra hot habenero, sweet & simple, chardonnay splash, spicy sweet, triple pepper, and many, many more. They also share great tips on different smoking woods to use, preparation prior to smoking your fish, canning smoked salmon, their favorite recipes using smoked salmon, and a section on troubleshooting meant to answer basic questions. If you like smoked salmon, you need this book. 6 x 9 inches, 180 pages.

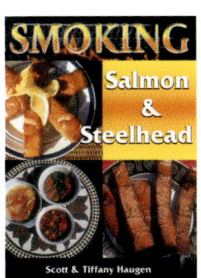

Spiral SB: $24.95
ISBN: 1-57188-290-1
UPC: 0-81127-00119-4
Available March 2005

PLANK COOKING:
THE ESSENCE OF NATURAL WOOD
Scott & Tiffany Haugen

From elegant restaurants to backyard grills, the ancient method of cooking food on a wooden plank is a cooking style that's rapidly growing in popularity. When it comes to capturing the essence of natural wood and unparalleled texture in meats, vegetables, and other culinary delights, nothing compares to plank cooking. In Plank Cooking: The Essence of Natural Wood, globe-trotting authors, Scott & Tiffany Haugen, share some of the world's most exquisite flavors. Thai red curry prawns, Achiote pork roast, pesto couscous stuffed chicken, and caramelized bananas are just a few of the unique recipes brought to life in this fully illustrated, one-of-a-kind book. In the oven or on a grill, plank cooking is fun and simple. This book outlines how to master the art of plank cooking—from seasoning planks to detailed cooking tips in over 100 easy-to-follow recipes. So whether you're hosting a large backyard BBQ, or just trying to satisfy the finicky eaters in your family, you will find many great meals in Plank Cooking. 6 x 9 inches, 152 pages.

Spiral SB: $19.95
ISBN: 1-57188-332-0
UPC: 0-81127-00164-4

SUMMER STEELHEAD FISHING TECHNIQUES
Scott Haugen

Scott Haugen is quickly becoming known for his fact-filled, full-color fishing books. This time Haugen explores summer steelhead, including: understanding summer steelhead; reading water; bank, drift, and sight fishing; jigs, plugs, lures, dragging flies, and bait; fishing high, turbid waters; tying your own leaders; egg cures; gathering bait; do-it-yourself sinkers; hatchery and recycling programs; mounting your catch; cleaning and preparation; smoking your catch; and more. 6 x 9 inches, 135 pages.

SB: $15.95
ISBN: 1-57188-295-2
UPC: 0-81127-00125-5

COOKING SALMON & STEELHEAD: EXOTIC RECIPES FROM AROUND THE WORLD
By Scott & Tiffany Haugen

This is not your grandmother's salmon cookbook. The long-time favorites are included and also unique yet easy-to-prepare dishes, like Cabo fish tacos and Tuscan pesto. This cookbook includes: Appetizers, soups & salads, entrees, one-dish meals, exotic tastes, marinades & rubs, outdoor cooking, pastas, stuffed fish, plank cooking, wine selection, scaling and fileting your catch, choosing market fish, cooking tips, and so much more. The Haugens have traveled to and studied cuisines in countries around the world—including the Caribbean, Asia, and Europe—your kitchen is not complete without a copy of Cooking Salmon & Steelhead.

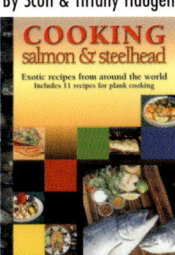

Spiral SB: $24.95
ISBN: 1-57188-291-X
UPC: 0-81127-00120-0

EGG CURES:
Proven Recipes & Techniques
Scott Haugen

Of all the natural baits, many consider eggs to be the best. Before this book, you'd have an easier time getting the secret recipe for Coca-Cola than getting a fisherman to part with his personal egg cure. But now, Scott Haugen has done it for you, he went to the experts—fishermen and fishing guides—to get their favorite egg cures and fishing techniques, plus their secret tricks and tips. The result is this book. These 28 recipes come from anglers who catch fish—read this book and you will too. Guaranteed! 5 1/2 x 8 1/2 inches, 90 pages.

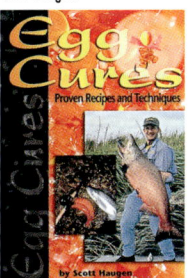

SB: $15.00
ISBN: 1-57188-238-3
UPC: 0-66066-00492-5

Spectacular photography and in-depth local knowledge highlight these useful fly-fishing guides; many fly-fishers are enjoying the enormously popular "Blue-Ribbon Fly-Fishing Guide" series. Each full-color book is filled with information on the fly-fishing in a particular state, including: successful techniques; productive flies and their patterns; hatch information; reading water; fish species; conservation issues; fly plates; local resources; map; and so much more. Useful and attractive, these guides are perfect for both visiting and local anglers. 8 1/2 x 11; Full color; 80 to 100 pages.

Michigan, Bob Linsenman - SB: $24.95
ISBN: 1-57188-160-3
UPC: 0-66066-00358-4

Ontario, Scott Smith - SB: $24.95
ISBN: 1-57188-162-X
UPC: 0-66066-00360-7

Wisconsin, R. Chris Halla - SB: $24.95
ISBN: 1-57188-161-1
UPC: 0-66066-00359-1

Ask for these books at your local fishing or book store or order from:
1-800-541-9498 (8 to 5 P.S.T.) • www.amatobooks.com
Frank Amato Publications, Inc. P.O. Box 82112 • Portland, Oregon 97282

Also Available from Frank Amato Publications

COLOR GUIDE TO STEELHEAD DRIFT FISHING
Bill Herzog

Each year nearly 1,000,000 steelhead are hooked in North America and the great majority of these fish are hooked using drift fishing techniques. This lavishly illustrated, all-color guide is the "bible" if you want to get in on the action. Written by one of America's greatest drift fishermen, you will learn the techniques that can guarantee your entry into the 10% of the anglers who hook 90% of the steelhead. This is a heavy-duty graduate course! 8 1/2 x 11 inches, 80 pages.

SB: $16.95
ISBN: 1-878175-59-9
UPC: 0-66066-00150-4

SPOON FISHING FOR STEELHEAD
Bill Herzog

One of the most effective ways to hook steelhead (and salmon) is with a spoon. Bill Herzog covers spoon fishing techniques for the full year, going into finishes, sizes, weights, shapes, water temperature differences, winter and summer fish differences, commercial and custom spoons, spoon parts suppliers, and reading water. Scores of color photos enhance the book, along with many line drawings, graphs and illustrations. 8 1/2 x 11 inches, 64 pages.

SB: $14.95
ISBN: 1-878175-30-0
UPC: 0-66066-00119-1

SPINNER FISHING FOR STEELHEAD, SALMON & TROUT
Jed Davis

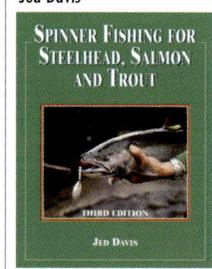

The "bible" for spinner fishing and the most in-depth, non-fly-fishing book ever written about steelhead and their habits. Information on how to make spinners is complete, including how to assemble, obtain parts, even how to silver plate. The fishing techniques, lure, line color and size selection, and reading fish-holding water sections are excellent. 8 1/2 x 11 inches, 97 pages.

SB: $19.95
ISBN: 0-936608-40-4
UPC: 0-66066-00056-9

ANCHOR FISHING FOR SALMON AND STEELHEAD
with Eric Linde and Carmen Macdonald

Two videos in one: how to anchor and how to catch salmon and steelhead on anchor. In this 75-minute production you will learn from the experts how to catch salmon and steelhead from an anchored boat. This time-proven fishing method can be practiced in any river. It is particularly effective in large rivers or during high flows in smaller rivers. In general, you will be provided the tools to become a better boatman and angler. 75 minutes

DVD: $29.95
ISBN: 1-57188-328-2
UPC: 0-81127-00167-5
VIDEO: $29.95
ISBN: 1-57188-315-0
UPC: 0-81127-00148-4

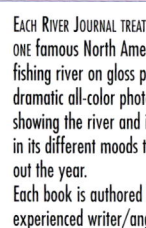

EACH RIVER JOURNAL TREATS IN-DEPTH ONE famous North American fly-fishing river on gloss paper with dramatic all-color photographs showing the river and its fishing in its different moods throughout the year.
Each book is authored by one experienced writer/angler; color photographs are contributed by professionals. Helpful area maps provide access information for anglers including river drifting, campgrounds, boat launching, shuttling, etc. There is insider fly-fishing help including timing of insect hatches, matching flies, lodging, guide and fly shop services, additional bibliography, map sources, phone numbers and addresses.
8 1/2 x 11 inches, 48 pages.

Grand River (MI) ISBN: 1-57188-277-4
SB: $15.95
UPC: 0-66066-00511-3
Grand River (MI) ISBN: 1-57188-278-2
HB: $30.00

STEELHEAD & SALMON DRIFT-FISHING TECHNIQUES
Timothy Kusherets

This comprehensive book goes way beyond the basics of drift-fishing techniques to include marine biology, ichthyology, meteorology, and physics as they apply to fish and fishing. Kusherets covers: species identification and anatomy; gear; set-ups; reading water; different drifting styles and techniques; understanding fish; spotting fish; troubleshooting; using the Internet; filleting your catch; extensive glossary; and more. The unique book will bring more fish to your line.
6 x 9 inches, 96 pages.

SB: $16.95
ISBN: 1-57188-300-2
UPC: 0-81127-00134-7

STEELHEAD DRIFT FISHING
with Bill Herzog and Nick Amato

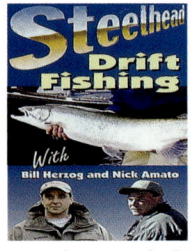

Bill Herzog and Nick Amato will show you how to catch one of the world's favorite game fish. Not one, but two native winter steelhead pushing the 20-pound mark are hooked and released!
This tape will teach you everything you need to know to experience the thrill of hooking giant sea-run rainbow trout.
Subjects covered include: Seasons, range and types; reading water and decoding rivers; terminal gear and rigging; techniques for steelhead drift fishing; natural baits; and the tools—rods, reels, lines and other personal gear. 60 minutes.

DVD: $25.00
ISBN: 1-57188-335-5
UPC: 0-81127-00169-9
VIDEO: $25.00
ISBN: 1-57188-228-6
UPC: 0-0-66066-00482-6

FLOAT FISHING FOR STEELHEAD
with Nick, Rob, and Matt

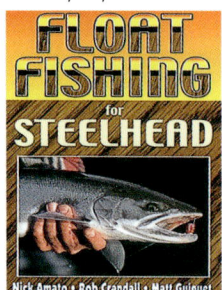

Float-fishing for steelhead is very productive. It's the easiest and most effective way to hook steelhead. Nick Amato, Rob Crandall, and Canadian float-fishing expert Matt Guiguet, share the secrets for successful float-fishing. They cover: Rigging floats, jigs, and gear; fishing techniques and tips; equipment; reading water; and more. If you are looking to hook more steelhead, look no further. 60 minutes.

DVD: $25.00
ISBN: 1-57188-331-2
UPC: 0-81127-00168-2
VIDEO: $25.00
ISBN: 1-57188-249-9
UPC: 0-66066-00502-1

SIDE-DRIFTING FOR STEELHEAD
Nick Amato and Mike Peruse

Side-drifting for steelhead and salmon is becoming one of the most popular angling methods used on the West Coast. This instructional video will show you how to quickly master the techniques necessary to side-drift effectively from a drift boat, jet boat or the bank. Subjects covered include: Boat handling and positioning, reading water, terminal tackle, rods and reels, sinker types, bait and boating etiquette. Nick and Mike get numerous steelhead on film—from strike to release. Whether you are an expert or novice side-drifter this DVD will get you revved up to get on the water! 60 minutes.

DVD: $25.00
ISBN: 1-57188-353-3
UPC: 0-81127-00187-3
Available October 2004

Ask for these books at your local fishing or book store or order from:
1-800-541-9498 (8 to 5 P.S.T.) • www.amatobooks.com
Frank Amato Publications, Inc. P.O. Box 82112 • Portland, Oregon 97282